MW01698385

Keys to Early Writing

Joan Sedita

Contributing Editors:

Lisa Klein

Donna Mastrovito

Melisa Rice

Keys to Literacy

319 Newburyport Tpke, Suite 205
Rowley, MA 01969
www.keystoliteracy.com

Author: Joan Sedita
Contributing Editors: Lisa Klein, Donna Mastrovito, Melisa Rice

ISBN 0-9786106-5-2 Printed in the United States of America

Published and Distributed by

Keys to Literacy

319 Newburyport Turnpike, Suite 205
Rowley, MA 01969
Phone: 978-948-8511 Email: info@keystoliteracy.com
www.keystoliteracy.com

Table of Contents

Introduction

This book is aligned to the content of the *Keys to Early Writing* professional development course developed by Keys to Literacy. *Keys to Early Writing* is designed for educators who teach beginning writing skills to students in grades K-2 and students in grades 3-5 who have difficulty with writing.

What is *Keys to Early Writing*?

Keys to Early Writing presents a framework for evidence-based writing instruction in kindergarten through grade 2. It includes suggestions for differentiation and scaffolds to support students who need extra support. Therefore, educators who provide supplemental or intervention writing instruction to struggling writers in grades three to five will also find the instructional practices helpful. *Keys to Early Writing* is aligned to state literacy standards, and connections are made to grade-specific Common Core writing, reading, language, and speaking and listening standards throughout the book.

Keys to Early Writing is not a writing program or curriculum. Rather, it provides the foundational knowledge teachers need to teach beginning writing skills to young students regardless of the published writing program or curriculum used in the schools where they teach. The framework includes the instructional topics listed below, represented in the book chapters. Combined, these topics constitute a complete approach to teaching beginning writing to students in the primary grades.

- **Writing Basics:** instructional framework, early writing development, teaching principles, spelling and handwriting
- **Writing Community:** writing environment, oral language as a foundation, daily opportunities to write, writing lesson routine.
- **The Writing Process:** think and plan, write, and think stages, collaboration, conferencing and feedback
- **Writing Craft and Structure:** using mentor text, text structure for the three types of writing (informational, opinion, narrative)
- **Drawing, Labels, Lists:** drawing as first steps to writing, oral rehearsal and dictation, lists and labels, linking to spelling and handwriting
- **Syntax, Sentences:** sentence parts, four types of sentences, activities for developing syntactic awareness
- **Paragraph Writing:** paragraph structure to support comprehension and writing, paragraph scaffolds, patterns of organization and transitions
- **Writing from Sources:** using prompts to write about content, shared research and writing

Keys to Early Writing translates the existing research about effective beginning writing instruction into practical teaching suggestions that can be integrated during time designated for writing instruction and throughout the rest of the school day. Research references are provided throughout.

The professional development goal for educators reading this book is to learn instructional practices that:

- address the requirements of state literacy standards for primary grades
- help students develop their oral language as a bridge to written expression
- develop proficient writers who use writing to communicate, including authentic writing for real purposes
- help students see themselves as competent, motivated writers
- teach students basic writing skills, strategies, and techniques
- teach students to integrate multiple writing skills to become skilled writers in later grades

Professional Development Information

Educators, schools and districts interested in accessing *Keys to Early Writing* professional development should contact Keys to Literacy.

Keys to Literacy has face-to-face, live-virtual, facilitated-online, and asynchronous online options for *Keys to Early Writing* professional development. For more information, please contact us or visit our website.

Keys to Literacy
info@keystoliteracy.com
www.keystoliteracy.com

Chapter 1
Writing Basics

The Writing Rope: A K-12 Instructional Framework

What skills are needed to become a skilled writer?

The Writing Rope (Sedita, 2019) is an instructional framework for teaching writing across all grades that identifies five components of writing skills that students must learn to become skilled writers: 1) Critical Thinking, 2) Syntax, 3) Text Structure, 4) Writing Craft, and 5) Transcription. The model uses a rope metaphor to represent the five strands that contribute to fluent, skilled writing. Figure 1-1 is a graphic representation of *The Writing Rope* framework. The components (i.e., strands) in the rope are explained in the left column of Figure 1-2 with descriptions of how each strand is addressed in *Keys to Early Writing* for teaching students in primary grades.

Figure 1-1

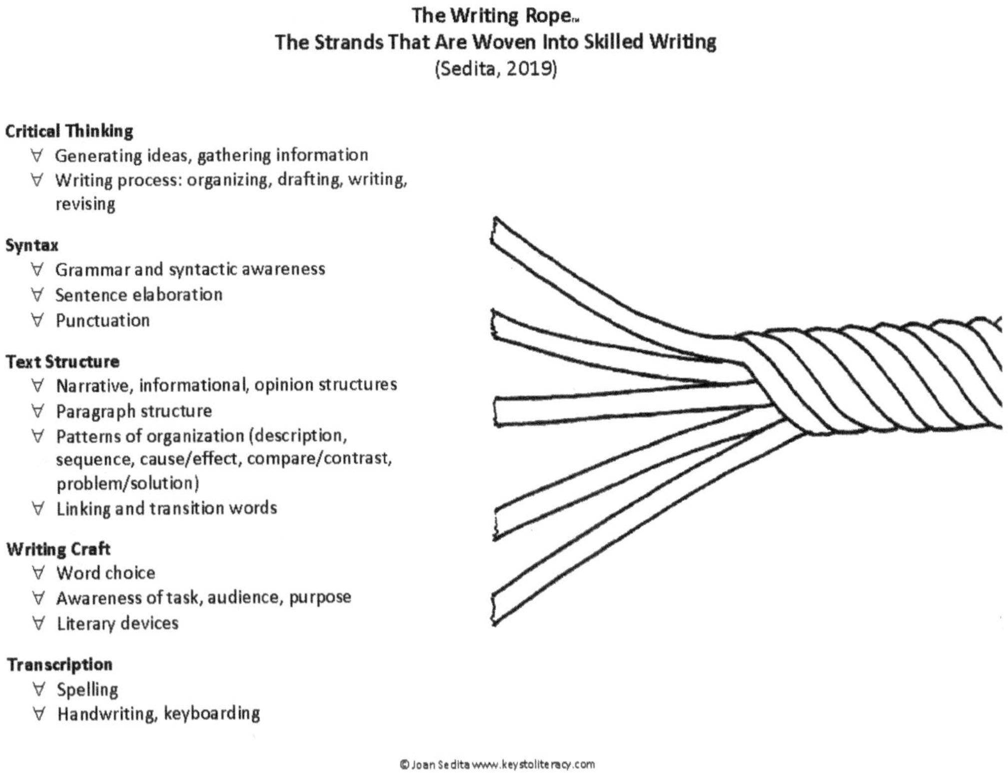

Figure 1-2

The Writing Rope

The Critical Thinking Strand	
This strand draws significantly on critical thinking and executive function skills, as well as the ability to develop background knowledge about a writing topic. Students engage in critical thinking as they think about what they want to communicate through their writing. If they are composing an informational or opinion piece, they may need to tap into comprehension skills to gather information from sources. This strand also includes awareness of the *writing process* (i.e., thinking, planning, drafting, writing, revising). For the thinking stage, students benefit from explicit instruction for brainstorming strategies and skills for gathering information from written and multi-media sources, such as note taking. They also need to learn planning strategies for organizing their thoughts, including the use of prewriting graphic organizers. Students need to be metacognitive and purposeful about working recursively through the stages of the writing process, and they benefit from explicit instruction in revising and editing strategies.	**Application to Primary Grades** Critical thinking for writing focuses on responding to text that is read or heard during read aloud. Writing is used to reinforce learning anything that is *read, said, or done* in all subjects throughout the school day. It is also about young students making choices about what they want to say. The basic stages in the writing process can be introduced to young children and highlighted whenever students compose using drawings or words. This part of the rope is addressed in Chapters 3 and 8. Chapter 3 specifically addresses the writing process.

The Syntax Strand	
Individual sentences communicate ideas that add up to make meaning. Efficient processing of sentence structure is necessary for listening and reading comprehension, as well as for communicating information and ideas in writing. *Syntax* is the study and understanding of grammar: the system and arrangement of words, phrases and clauses that make up a sentence. Students develop syntactic awareness as they learn the correct use and relationship of words in sentences. This begins with exposure to standard English by listening to people talk, and reading or listening to written text. Students benefit from explicit instruction focused on building sentence skills, including activities such as sentence elaboration and sentence combining.	**Application to Primary Grades** Young children benefit from explicit instruction about basic sentence structure, including the parts of a sentence and how to expand their sentences through sentence elaboration practice. They also benefit from activities that develop syntactic awareness including sentence scrambles and sentence combining. This part of the rope is addressed specifically in Chapter 6.

<table>
<tr><th colspan="2">The Text Structure Strand</th></tr>
<tr><td>

- Text structure is unique to written language, and awareness of several levels of text structure supports both writing and reading comprehension. Students benefit from explicit instruction about levels of text structure.
- <u>Narrative, informational, and opinion text structure:</u> knowledge of the different organization structures for these three types of writing, including the use of introductions, body development, and conclusions
- <u>Paragraph structure:</u> understanding that written paragraphs are used to *chunk* text into manageable units that are organized around a central idea and supporting details
- <u>Patterns of organization:</u> understanding that sentences and paragraphs can be organized to convey a specific purpose including *description, sequence, cause and effect, compare and contrast, problem and solution*
- <u>Transition words or phrases:</u> ability to use words or phrases to link sentences, paragraphs, or sections of text – including knowledge of transitions associated with specific patterns of organization

</td><td>

Application to Primary Grades

The three main types of writing (informational, narrative, opinion) can be introduced in primary grades, including basic examples of introductions and conclusions. Initially, drawings with some words are used to represent these genres, leading to paragraph writing by the end of grade 2.

Patterns of organization, along with simple examples of associated transitions, can also be introduced.

Teachers should encourage students to read like a writer to see the reciprocal relationship of text structure between reading and writing.

Chapters 4 and 7 address these levels of text structure.

</td></tr>
</table>

<table>
<tr><th colspan="2">The Writing Craft Strand</th></tr>
<tr><td>

This strand addresses skills and strategies often referred to as *writer's craft* or *writer's moves.* This includes a number of techniques that writers employ that affect writing style, text structure, and choice of words. Students benefit from explicit instruction in the following:

- <u>Word choice:</u> purposeful use of specific vocabulary, word placement, and dialogue to convey meaning and create an effect on the reader
- <u>Writer's voice:</u> the techniques and style of writing an author uses to show emotion, personality, or point of view

</td><td>

Application to Primary Grades

The concept of writer's craft can be introduced in the early grades, including basic techniques such as the use of illustrations and layout of visuals on the page, use of font type and size, organizing features such as headings and captions, and the use of dialogue and speech bubbles.

The concept of the *writer's voice* can also be introduced using simple examples found in read aloud books.

</td></tr>
</table>

• Literary devices: understanding and use of common literary elements (e.g., plot, setting, narrative, characters, theme) and literary techniques (e.g., imagery, personification, figurative language, alliteration, allegory, irony) When teachers share examples of mentor text that include clear examples of how authors use techniques, students are better able to imitate them in their own writing. This strand also addresses the importance of being mindful of the task, audience, and purpose when writing. Awareness of these elements influences decisions about word choice, tone, length, and style of a writing piece.	This part of the rope is addressed in Chapter 4.

The Transcription Strand	
This strand addresses spelling and handwriting/keyboarding skills. They are basic skills that are needed to transcribe the words a writer wants to put into writing. Once students become automatic and fluent with spelling and handwriting/keyboarding, they can focus their attention on the other strands of the writing rope. If students do not develop fluency with these skills by grade 3, this will put a constraint on writing development as they move into the later grades.	**Application to Primary Grades** Spelling and handwriting are best taught as part of phonics instruction. *Keys to Early Writing* focuses on oral and written composing, and therefore does not provide in-depth instructional suggestions for teaching spelling and handwriting. The role of transcription skills is addressed in Chapters 1 and 6.

The *Not So Simple View of Writing*

The *Not So Simple View of Writing*, shown in Figure 1-3, is a developmental model for writing that highlights several processes and skills that support writing (Berninger & Winn, 2006). In addition to transcription skills and composing (text generation), students must have sufficient executive function abilities to write, including attention, the ability to set goals, planning and revising, and self-regulation to be able to monitor themselves while writing. Working memory, the ability to hold onto ideas and information, is at the center of the model. Without working memory, writers cannot hold on to what they want to say long enough to be able to decide which words and sentences to write and how to spell those words.

Figure 1-3

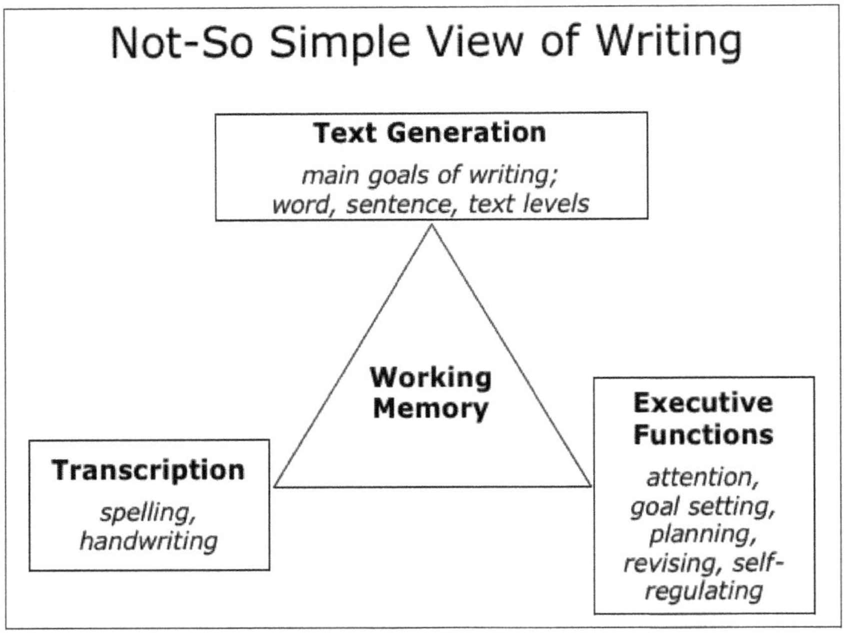

What do we know about writing in K-2?

The National Council of Teachers of English (NCTE) notes the following about writing in the primary grades:

- Young children possess knowledge about written language and a variety of forms of writing – stories, lists, signs – from an early age.
- The "language arts" develop in concert. Reading supports writing, drawing supports writing, and writing supports reading. Opportunities to use multiple expressions of language increases language ability.
- Writing is a social activity and writing instruction should be embedded into social contexts. Through face-to-face interactions, children come to understand that writing serves many functions, that relationships exist between speaking and writing, and that writing is aimed at, and therefore must be sensitive to, an audience.
- Writing can be an effective tool for thinking and learning throughout the school day, in all subjects.
- Writing develops in non-linear ways and takes multiple forms before becoming conventional. The sophistication of children's ideas and their understanding of language are not always reflected in their written forms.

The research report *Teaching Elementary School Students to Be Effective Writers* (Graham et al., 2012) makes these points:

> "Writing is a fundamental part of engaging in professional, social, community, and civic activities. Because writing is a valuable tool for communication, learning, and self-expression, people who do not have adequate writing skills may be at a disadvantage and may face restricted opportunities for education and employment. Students should develop an early foundation in writing in order to communicate their ideas effectively and efficiently – yet many American students are not strong writers. In fact, less than one-third of all students performed at or above the "proficient" level in writing on the 2007 National Assessment of Educational Progress Writing Assessment." (p. 6) *Updated Note: only 27% of grade 8 and grade 12 students performed at or above the proficient level on the 2011 NAEP writing assessment.*

Because writing is essential to success in school and beyond, writing instruction must be an important part of an elementary school literacy curriculum. For children in the early elementary grades, the goal should be developing basic skills to learn how to write, as well as to begin using writing to learn.

It is sometimes assumed that writing is simply the reverse side of reading, and as young children learn to read, they will naturally learn to write. However, while reading and writing are complementary, students in kindergarten through grade two require dedicated time and explicit instruction to learn how to write. Through this instruction, young students will

- learn how to use writing to communicate;
- learn and practice basic writing skills, strategies and techniques;
- and learn how to integrate multiple writing components to become skilled writers in later grades.

Writing Development in the Primary Grades

Writing, like reading, should be defined from a developmental standpoint, which begins with the acquisition of foundational skills, and then leads to application of more sophisticated techniques. There is wide variation between the writing ability and skills of kindergarten students and students in grade two, and there is wide variation of writing ability among students within the same grade. It is not easy to meet the needs of individual students in a class that includes students with a wide range of skills.

There is a progression of developmental stages that typical students follow as they move from kindergarten through grade 2. At first, young students may only be able to draw and compose orally, adding symbols that look like letters to their drawings. As they learn how letters represent sounds that can be combined to write words, they begin to add labels, lists, phrases, and sentences to their drawings. Once they can write sentences, they can write different types of text for specific purposes. This includes learning the three main types of writing (genres) required in many state literacy standards: informational, narrative, opinion.

State Literacy Standards

Most states in the United States have adopted the Common Core State Standards (2010) or a similar set of standards. While writing instruction has always been a part of early literacy curricula, it did not receive as much attention as reading did after the National Reading Panel report was published in 2000 (NICHH). That has changed in recent years, partially due to the emphasis placed on writing in the ten Common Core anchor writing standards that are addressed in kindergarten through grade 12. *Keys to Early Writing* is tightly aligned to these standards, and connections to writing, reading, speaking and listening, and language skills for kindergarten through grade 2 are made throughout this book.

There are ten writing anchor standards in the Common Core, organized into four categories. In addition, there are standards from the other literacy components that are related to early writing instruction. Anchor standards and the grade-specific requirements for Kindergarten through grade 3 for writing-related standards are listed in the Appendix.

Technology

Common Core writing standard #6 addresses the role of technology in writing. The description of this standard for kindergarten through grade 2 is:

> "With guidance and support from adults, use/explore a variety of digital tools to produce and publish writing including collaboration with peers."

Most children in primary grades are not developmentally ready to master keyboarding skills. However, with guidance from adults, they can begin to learn many of the features that older writers use to produce writing such as drag-and-drop and cut-and-paste. The selection of hardware, software, and applications that can be used to support all stages of the writing process is constantly growing.

Research-Based Instructional Practices

Researchers and practitioners have been studying writing instruction for many decades to identify effective instructional practices. It is important for teachers to be aware of this research so that the decisions they make about teaching writing take into account what others have learned about best practices.

General Research Findings

There are several teaching practices that consistently come up as effective across numerous research studies, listed in Figure 1-4.

Figure 1-4

General Writing Research Findings

- Teach students that there are different purposes for writing.
- Assign writing tasks for real audiences that are relevant to students' everyday lives.
- Teach the stages of the writing process.
- Explicitly teach writing skills, strategies, techniques.
- Provide procedural scaffolds.
- Provide opportunities for students to collaborate with peers and the teacher.
- Use mentor models for students to emulate.
- Provide feedback.
- Increase the amount students write and time spent on writing instruction.
- Create a supportive, engaging writing environment.

Sources: Hidi & Boscolo, 2006; Chapman, 2006; Donovan & Smolkin, 2006; Boscolo & Gelati, 2007; Coker, 2007; MacArthur, 2007; Pritchard & Honeycutt, 2007

Research Specific to Elementary Writing Instruction

There are two research reports based on meta-analyses of research on effective elementary writing instruction that are referenced throughout this book. The findings from both are provided in Figures 1-5 and 1-6.

Figure 1-5

Teaching Elementary Students to be Effective Writers: A Practice Guide (Graham et al., 2012)

This report was published by the U.S. Department of Education's Institute of Education Sciences. The report reviews studies related to effective practices for teaching writing to students in kindergarten through grade five.

Recommendations

1. **Provide daily time for students to write.**

2. **Teach students to use the writing process for a variety of purposes.**

   2a Teach students the writing process.
   1. Teach students strategies for the various components of the writing process.
   2. Gradually release writing responsibility from the teacher to the student.
   3. Guide students to select and use appropriate writing strategies.
   4. Encourage students to be flexible in their use of the components of the writing process.

2b Teach students to write for a variety of purposes.
1. Help students understand the different purposes of writing.
2. Help expand students' concept of audience.
3. Teach students to emulate the features of good writing.
4. Teach students techniques for writing effectively for different purposes.

3. Teach students to become fluent with handwriting, spelling, sentence construction, typing, and word processing.
1. Teach very young writers how to hold a pencil correctly and form letters fluently and efficiently.
2. Teach students to spell words correctly.
3. Teach students to construct sentences for fluency, meaning, and style.
4. Teach students to type fluently and to use a word processor to compose.

4. Create an engaged community of writers.
1. Teachers should participate as members of the community by writing and sharing their writing.
2. Give students writing choices.
3. Encourage students to collaborate as writers.
4. Provide students with opportunities to give and receive feedback throughout the writing process.
5. Publish students' writing and extend the community beyond the classroom.

Figure 1-6

Research-Based Writing Practices and the Common Core:
Meta-analysis and Meta-synthesis
(Graham, Harris, Santangelo, 2015)

This article summarizes research-supported practices that can be used to meet Common Core State Standards writing objectives in kindergarten to grade eight. These practices were identified by conducting a meta-analysis of writing intervention studies and the practices of exceptional literacy teachers.

Recommendations

1. Create a Writing Environment That is Positive and Supportive

Given the demands of state writing standards, it is important to develop a writing environment that is motivating, pleasant, and nonthreatening, where teachers support students and their writing efforts, and students support each other.

2. Establish Writing Routines That Create a Pleasant and Motivating Writing Environment

It is helpful to establish routines and create a positive classroom where students share their work with others, are encouraged to try hard, and are motivated to write.

3. Implement a Process Approach to Writing

A *process approach* to writing includes creating a pleasant and positive writing environment, promoting high levels of student interactions to support writing, writing for real audiences and authentic purposes, stressing personal responsibility and ownership of writing projects, and encouraging self-reflection and evaluation. This type of model was found to have a positive effect on the quality of writing produced by students in grades 1 to 8.

4. Create Routines That Ensure Students Write Frequently

The basic premise is that students must write frequently if they are to grow as writers. Research finds that when teachers increased how frequently students in grades 2-8 wrote, there was a corresponding improvement in the quality of their writing. It also finds that for students in grades 2-6, extra writing made students better readers.

5. Design Instructional Routines Where Students Compose Together

Having students work together when writing is an effective practice. A common characteristic of studies that tested collaborative writing was that students were provided with specific directions for what to do when working together and then taught how to carry out these guidelines.

6. Establish Goals for Students' Writing

Research finds that writing quality is enhanced when teachers set high, but realistic expectations for students' writing. This includes setting clear, specific, and reasonably challenging goals for student writing.

7. Use Twenty-First-Century Writing Tools

Word processors have a number of advantages over writing by hand, as electronic text is legible, and it can easily be deleted, added, rewritten, or moved. Research finds that the quality of writing of students in grades 1 to 8 who used word processing versus writing by hand improved.

8. Provide Feedback

Research finds that the use of formative assessment, (teacher, peer, and self-assessment) improved children's writing. When teachers monitor students' progress as writers they can adjust classroom practices to meet the collective as well as the individual needs of their students.

9. Ensure Students Acquire Needed Writing Skills, Knowledge, and Strategies

Research supports teaching writing skills (e.g., handwriting, spelling, grammar and usage), attributes of specific types of text (e.g., opinion, informative, narrative) and writing strategies that support planning, revising and editing.

10. Teach Foundational Writing Skills

Research finds that teaching spelling and handwriting to grade 1 to 3 students enhanced the overall quality of their writing. It also finds that teaching sentence construction through sentence-combining improves the quality of student writing.

11. Increase Students' Knowledge About Writing

Three types of knowledge that are important are knowledge about the writing topic, knowledge about genre, and knowledge about the words used to convey meaning. Research supports the following:

- Have students gather ideas and information to write about through prewriting activities such as locating writing content through brainstorming, reading, drawing, and/or by using graphic organizers.
- Teach students the basic elements of the different types of text (text structure).
- Provide students with good models of written text.
- Teach students vocabulary that will improve their text.

12. Teach Students Strategies for Planning, Drafting, Revising, and Editing

Research finds that it is beneficial for teachers to encourage students to employ a variety of planning, revising, and editing strategies to help them create and improve what they write. Research also supports the explicit teaching of strategies.

13. Use Writing as a Tool to Support Students' Learning

Research supports having students use writing as a tool for learning, including writing about content presented in class and writing about materials read. This results in improved comprehension of such material. Writing to learn activities include writing short answers to questions, taking notes, writing a summary, and writing more extended responses.

Teaching Principles

Teaching writing is a complex, multifaceted activity requiring teachers to juggle multiple goals, tasks, and student needs. The teaching principles listed in Figure 1-7 offer research-based instructional guidelines that support student learning when collectively used on a regular basis.

Figure 1-7

Gradual Release of Responsibility	Also referred to as an *I do it, We do it, You do it* approach to teaching. Includes explicit instruction using a direct and systematic approach, modeling, and think aloud to introduce and teach a new writing skill, strategy, or technique. (Pearson & Gallagher, 1983)
Systematic Instruction	Systematic instruction refers to a planned and logical sequence of teaching, proceeding in small steps and checking for student understanding before moving to the next step. Includes a writing scope and sequence that moves from drawing, to labeling and lists, to sentences, to paragraphs.
Differentiated Instruction	Differentiated instruction calls for designing instruction to suit individual student needs rather than using a standardized approach to instruction that assumes all students will learn to write the same way.
Scaffolding	Scaffolding is assistance offered by a teacher or a peer to support learning a writing skill that a student is initially unable to grasp independently, and then removing the assistance once the skill is learned. This is not the same as doing the work for the student. Scaffolding is a hallmark of differentiated instruction.
Use Multi-Sensory Activities	Teach writing skills by including activities that incorporate auditory, visual, tactile, and kinesthetic pathways for learning.
Automaticity Through Practice	When students learn a writing skill at an automatic (mastery) level, they have learned it so thoroughly that they can use it with little or no conscious attention. In particular, teachers should strive to develop automatic spelling and handwriting skills so students can focus their attention on the composing aspects of writing. Significant guided practice is an essential element of developing automaticity.

More About the Gradual Release of Responsibility

The *Gradual Release of Responsibility* model (Pearson & Gallagher, 1983) is a framework that is sometimes referred to as the *I do it, We do it, You do it* model of instruction. Using this approach, teachers gradually release responsibility to students to learn and apply a writing skill.

The teacher is the centerpiece of the *I do it* stage, employing an explicit and systematic approach that includes modeling and think aloud to introduce and teach a writing skill. At the *We do it* stage, students practice the skill in whole group or small groups. The teacher guides this practice and provides targeted, corrective feedback to students. During this stage, the teacher differentiates instructional support and provides scaffolds based on the individual needs of students. At the *You do it* stage, students are able to use the skill independently. The amount of guided practice that students need to reach the independent level varies from student to student. Figure 1-8 provides details.

Figure 1-8

Gradual Release of Responsibility: I, We, You Sequence

I	introduce, provide background knowledge	The teacher describes the skill, strategy or technique and explains what it is, how it works, and why it supports writing.
	model the strategy, use think aloud	The teacher models writing and how the skill, strategy or technique is used through shared, interactive writing that includes demonstration, think aloud, soliciting ideas from students, and providing examples.
We	collaborative use	Students collaborate in small groups to practice applying the skill, strategy, or technique. The teacher is the *guide on the side.*
	guided practice	Students practice the skill, strategy, or technique with assistance from the teacher as needed.
You	independent use	Students apply the skill, strategy, or technique independently.

Composing Versus Transcription Skills (Spelling, Handwriting)

As noted earlier in this chapter, handwriting and spelling are described as *transcription* skills. If spelling and handwriting are not fluent and require considerable effort, students cannot focus on higher level composing skills. One of the recommendations in the Institute of Education Science research report (Graham et al., 2012) is to teach students how to become fluent with handwriting and spelling.

Figure 1-9 identifies grade-level expectations for students, organized into two categories: composing skills and print concepts/transcription skills. Keep in mind that teachers may have children who have more- or less-advanced skills. It is important to differentiate instruction and use scaffolds to meet the individual needs of every student.

An overview of effective instruction for spelling is provided in this chapter, including a word-writing developmental sequence and information about invented spelling. This chapter also provides an overview of handwriting instruction. However, *Keys to Early Writing* does not provide detailed instructional suggestions for a phonics scope and sequence or spelling rules and principles which are best taught during phonics lessons. Educators can access additional professional development for teaching spelling through *Keys to Beginning Reading* professional development available from Keys to Literacy.

Figure 1-9

<table>
<tr><th>EXPECTATIONS
Composing Skills</th><th>EXPECTATIONS
Transcription Skills</th></tr>
<tr><th colspan="2">Kindergarten</th></tr>
<tr><td>• Composing is expressed primarily through speaking, dictating, or drawing.
• Students may attempt to write messages of their own and read them back.
• Students produce complete sentences when speaking.
• Students use frequently occurring nouns, verbs, and question words while composing.
• Students capitalize the first word when writing a sentence.</td><td>Students:
• Know that writing differs from drawing, has distinct letter forms, and can be read back
• Know how to write at least some letter forms
• Know that spaces are between words
• Know that writing goes from left to right and is organized from top to bottom of the page
• May or may not know the alphabetic principle and produce early phonetic spellings of some sounds in words</td></tr>
</table>

<table>
<tr><th colspan="2">Grade 1</th></tr>
<tr><td>• Composing is expressed primarily through speaking, drawing, words, and gradually written sentences.
• Students begin to produce the four types of sentences (declarative, interrogative, imperative, exclamatory) and compound sentences when speaking.
• Students use a wider variety of nouns, pronouns, conjunctions, prepositions, and verb tenses while composing.</td><td>Students:
• Know the alphabetic principle and spell by sound using alphabet letter names and sound-symbol correspondences
• Remember the spellings of commonly used high frequency words
• Begin to write words in sequence with word spaces, capitalize the first word, and use punctuation at the ends of sentences</td></tr>
</table>

• Students may be amenable to adding details to drawings and text in response to feedback from peers and adults.	

Grade 2	
• Composing is expressed primarily through speaking and writing sentences. • Students write compound and complex sentences, and all four types of sentences. • Students begin to link sentences into a basic paragraph. • There is more independence in generating ideas. • Students use more complicated forms of nouns and pronouns, irregular verbs, and a variety of adjectives and adverbs when composing. • Students begin to be aware of task, audience, purpose. • Students may be amenable to adding details and text revision in response to feedback from peers and adults.	• Spelling and handwriting are becoming more sufficient to focus more on the demands of composing. • Students apply basic capitalization. rules and begin using more punctuation (e.g., commas in letter greetings, apostrophe for contraction and possessives).

Grade 3	
• Composing is expressed primarily through writing. • Students write compound and complex sentences. • Students link sentences into multi-paragraphs. • Students use a wider range of vocabulary, including terms that represent abstract concepts when composing. • Students write with an awareness of task, audience, purpose. • Students revise writing with feedback support from peers and adults.	• Spelling and handwriting are sufficiently fluent to focus on the demands of composing. • Students use more complex punctuation (e.g., commas and quotation marks in dialogue).

Overview of Spelling Instruction

Research findings emphasize the importance of spelling for overall writing quality for students in early grades (Kim et al., 2011). However, spelling instruction should be more than having students memorize the spelling of individual words! Instruction needs to be provided in *orthography* – i.e., how the English writing system works. This means teaching students that letters and letter patterns represent the sounds of spoken English, which is called the *alphabetic principle*. It includes instruction to develop phonemic awareness, to learn phonics concepts, and to develop morphological awareness.

Research also finds that explicit spelling instruction is more effective than informal instruction, it supports both reading and spelling, and should be part of a strong writing curriculum (Graham & Santangelo, 2014; Coker & Ritchey, 2015).

English Spelling (Orthography) and Phonics Instruction

The English spelling system is alphabetic because we spell primarily using a system where letters represent spoken sounds. Learning the *alphabetic principle* means learning about the relationships between sounds and the letters that represent them.

Phonics instruction helps students use the alphabetic principle to learn those relationships by teaching how the 26 individual letters and letter combinations (graphemes) represent the 44 sounds (phonemes) in spoken English. Learning that there are predictable relationships between sounds and letters allows children to apply these relationships to both familiar and unfamiliar words and to begin to read and spell.

English Spelling Can Be Challenging

Learning to spell words is more difficult than learning to read words for several reasons.

- English spelling is not purely phonetic. There are many words that cannot be spelled phonetically, and this can be frustrating sometimes for young students. However, approximately 84% of English words are phonetically regular, so teaching the most common sound-spelling relationships is very useful (Hanna et al., 1966).

- Many speech sounds (especially vowel sounds) in English are represented by multiple spellings, so making the correct choice can be confusing.

- Some of the most common, high-frequency words are irregularly spelled (e.g., *the, of, was, are, have, said*). Students must be taught to memorize the irregularly spelled parts of these words.

Phonics Instruction: Decoding and Encoding

Decoding (reading words) is the process of converting printed words into their spoken forms by using phonics. **Encoding** (spelling words) is the process of using letter/sound knowledge to write words. Both require phonemic awareness and sound-letter knowledge. What we teach for decoding is used for spelling, and spelling reinforces decoding, which is why an effective phonics lesson should include time to use dictation to practice spelling words that include the phonics concept that is the focus of the lesson.

Spelling and Word-Writing Developmental Stages

As students progress from pre-school through grade 2, there is a developmental sequence that they follow as they move from basic scribbles that represent words to writing words (Gentry, 1982; Gentry, 2007; Cabell et al, 2013; Graves, 1989). Figure 1-10 presents the common stages of word-writing development across these ages.

Figure 1-10

Pre-K - K	**PRELITERATE** *drawing & scribbling*	Children write scribbles that look like a random assortment of marks. Through scribbling, the child explores space and form, and learns that symbols are used to create a permanent record of ideas and thoughts. 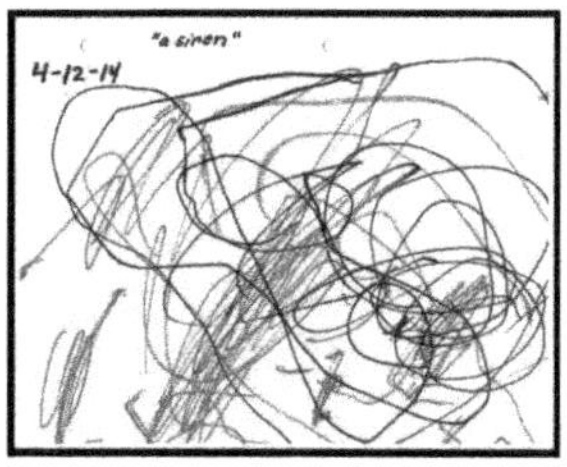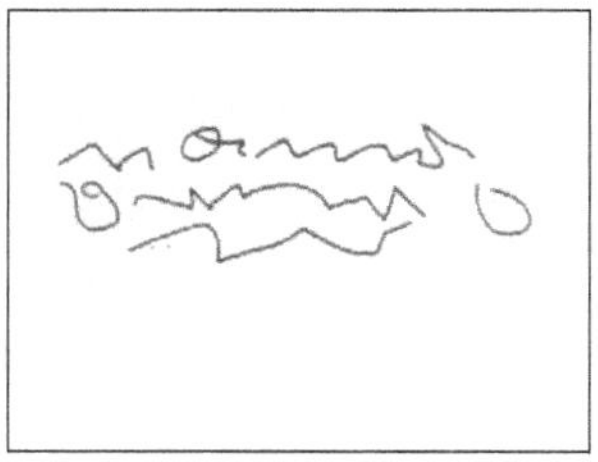
Pre-K - K	**EARLY EMERGENT** *letter-like symbols*	Children create symbols that look like letters as they display their understanding that writers use symbols to convey their meaning. 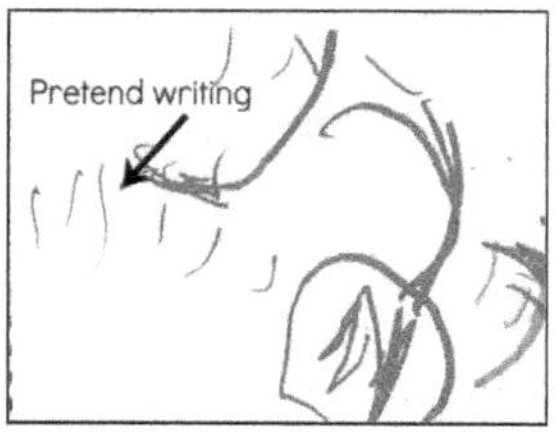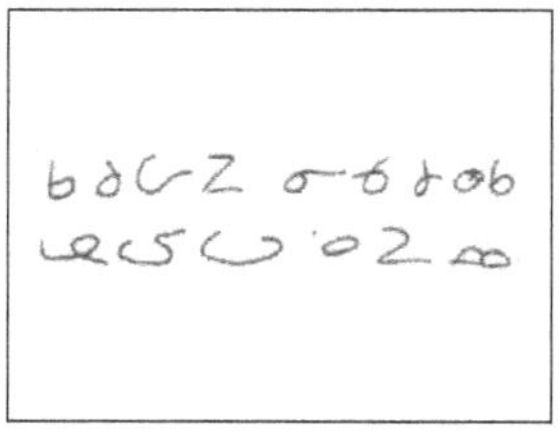

Pre-K - K	**EMERGENT, PRE-COMMUNICATIVE** *letters, strings of letters*	Children learn to write real letters. They use the letters randomly, especially letters in their names, often as strings of letters. There is a lack of sound-to-symbol correspondence between the words they are writing and the letters they are using. 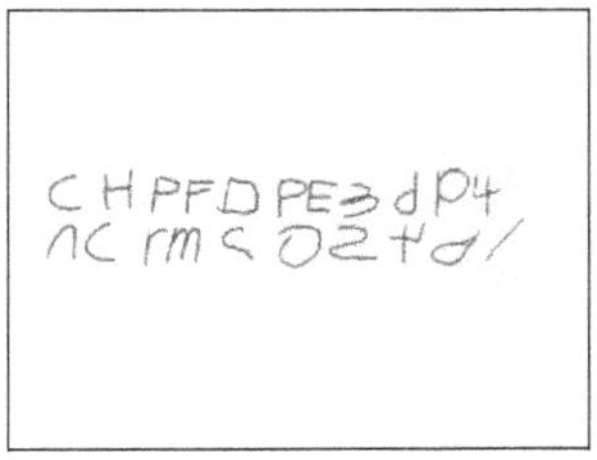
	SEMI-PHONETIC *some letter-sound correspondences*	Children begin to show they understand letter-sound correspondence and apply rudimentary logic using letters to represent words, sounds, and syllables. They start by writing the beginning sound of a word to represent the word. 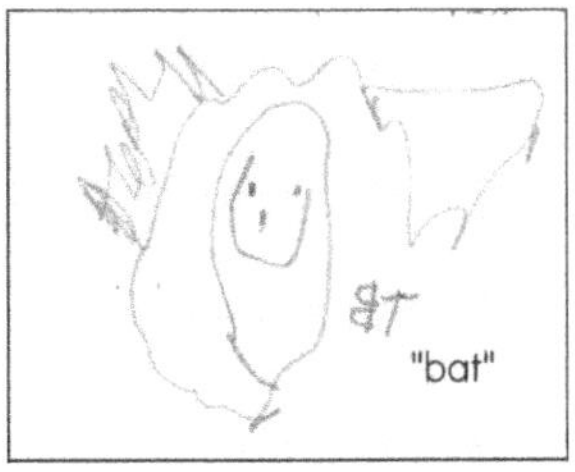

K - 1	**PHONETIC** *every sound represented*	Children use a letter or group of letters to represent every speech sound that they hear in a word. Although some of their choices do not conform to conventional English spelling, they are systematic and easily understood. Examples: *KOM* for *come*, *EN* for *in* 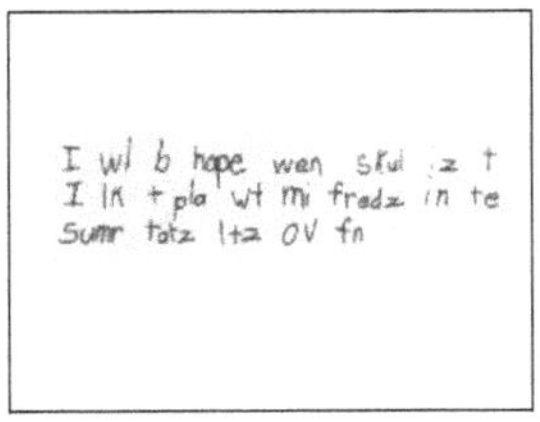

<table>
<tr>
<td></td>
<td>TRANSITIONAL
letters based on sound-symbol correspondence</td>
<td>Children begin to assimilate the conventional alternative for representing sounds, moving from a dependence on phonology (sound) for representing words to a reliance on visual representation and an understanding of the structure of words. Examples: EGUL for eagle, HIGHEKED for hiked
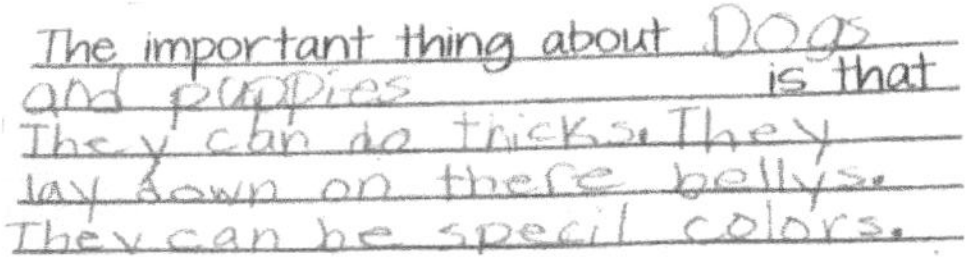
</td>
</tr>
<tr>
<td>1 - 2 +</td>
<td>SPELLING FLUENCY
conventional spelling</td>
<td>Children know the English orthographic system and its basic rules and understand how to deal with such things as prefixes and suffixes, silent consonants, alternative spellings, and irregular spellings.
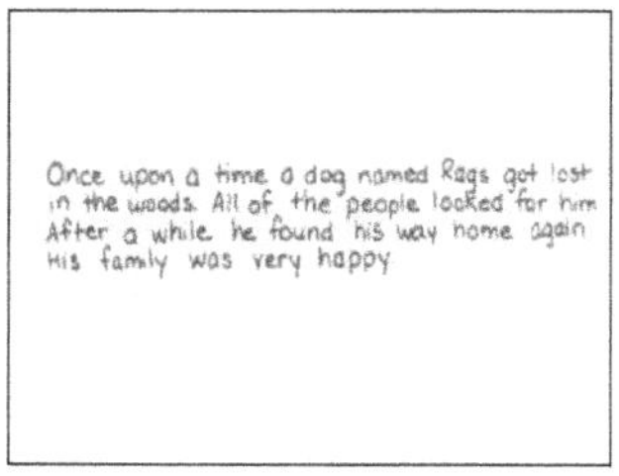
</td>
</tr>
<tr>
<td colspan="3">Adapted from: Gentry, 1982; Gentry, 2007, Cabell et al, 2013; Graves, 1989
Samples from: Salt Lake City School District; http://www.themeasuredmom.com/stages-of-writing-development-help-kids-move/</td>
</tr>
</table>

<u>*Invented Spelling*</u>

Invented spelling refers to young children's attempts to use their best judgments about spelling. Even at an early age, children are able to detect phonetic characteristics of words that English spelling represents. Coker & Ritchey (2015) note:

> "Sometimes these attempts barely resemble a word's conventional spelling. Invented spelling has long been seen as children's active attempts to understand the spelling system. It may be that engaging in invented spelling helps students explore the relationships between sounds and letters, and how they work together in words. As students' understanding of the spelling system grows, their use of invented spelling will fade. While we encourage teachers to support students' invented spelling efforts, we also believe that students should have models of correct spelling. This means that students' writing should have correct (or corrected) spelling when it is posted in the classroom." (pp 66-67)

By looking at the way students represent words when they attempt to write or label their drawings, teachers can find clues about their phonemic awareness abilities and knowledge of letter-sound correspondences. An informed teacher will recognize why young students use letters the way they do.

Examples

- What clues are provided in the spellings to the right by kindergarten and grade 1 students?
- What do these spellings tell you about their phonemic awareness and phonics skills?
- What would these spellings indicate if the students were in third, fourth, or fifth grade?

Suggested responses to these questions are provided at the end of this chapter.

pll **pool**	it **at**
fkl **freckle**	bns **bunch**
jrg **drag**	uor **you're**
wien **wishing**	pwtx **black**
fztz **fastest**	cwt **quiet**
pĕr **preacher**	KiB **clapping**
I no Tim mom Tim **I have a pet dog.**	

Overview of Handwriting Instruction

When students develop fluent handwriting skills, they can focus their attention on composing. Difficulty with handwriting can have negative consequences for later writing ability. Teaching handwriting should be an essential part of a writing curriculum. Stephen Graham (2009-2010) explains it this way:

> "Of all the knowledge and skills that are required to write, handwriting is the one that places the earliest constraints on writing development. If children cannot form letters – or cannot form them with reasonable legibility and speed – they cannot translate the language in their minds into written text. Struggling with handwriting can lead to a self-fulfilling prophecy in which students avoid writing, come to think of themselves as not being able to write, and fall further and further behind their peers." (p. 20)

> "Young writers typically cope with the multiple demands of handwriting and composing by minimizing the composing process (planning, organizing, etc.). Because so much of their thinking must be devoted to forming legible letters, they turn composing into a knowledge-telling process in which writing is treated as a forward-moving idea-generation activity. A relevant idea is generated and written down, with each new phrase or idea serving as the stimulus for the next one. Mostly absent from this approach to writing are more reflective and demanding thinking activities such as considering the constraints imposed by the topic, the needs of the reader, or the most coherent way to organize the text." (p. 21)

Related Literacy Standards

The Common Core State Standards addresses handwriting in the Language Standards:

- Kindergarten: Print many upper- and lowercase letters.
- Grade 1: Print all upper- and lowercase letters. `

Why teach handwriting?
(Graham, 2009-2010; Santangelo & Graham, 2014; Coker & Ritchey, 2015; Reutzel et al., 2017)

- Handwriting instruction produces significantly better writing quality and productivity. Students' sentence-writing skills, the amount they write, and the quality of their writing all improve along with their handwriting.
- Letter writing and fluency are related to both spelling and word reading. Handwriting supports and reinforces the learning of letter names and sound-letter correspondences.
- Teaching handwriting underscores the idea that writing is a communication tool and reminds students that they need to produce text that is legible for other readers.
- As students get older, the quality of their handwriting influences the way their writing is evaluated and graded.

Teaching Handwriting

There is significant research spanned over decades demonstrating that directly teaching handwriting enhances legibility and fluency (Graham 2009-2010; Peck et al., 1980). Handwriting instruction does not require a significant time investment, and opportunities to practice handwriting can be found throughout the school day. Based on research, Graham suggests that in kindergarten through grade 3, handwriting should be taught in short sessions several times a week or even daily, with 50 to 100 minutes a week devoted to its mastery.

There is wide variety in how writing is taught, the materials used, and the amount of time devoted to handwriting instruction. Coker and Ritchey (2015) identify three types of instructional practices:

- Explicit, systematic instruction using a handwriting curriculum or program: Formation of letters is taught daily following a scope and sequence determined by the curriculum.
- Integrated instruction taught in the context of a reading/spelling curriculum or program: Formation of letters is taught daily or less frequently using a combination of explicit and implicit instruction.
- Incidental instruction: Handwriting is taught and practiced on an as-needed basis with the teacher making decisions about when and how to teach handwriting.

There are three main aspects of handwriting instruction: pencil grasp, letter formation using writing strokes, and legibility.

Pencil Grip

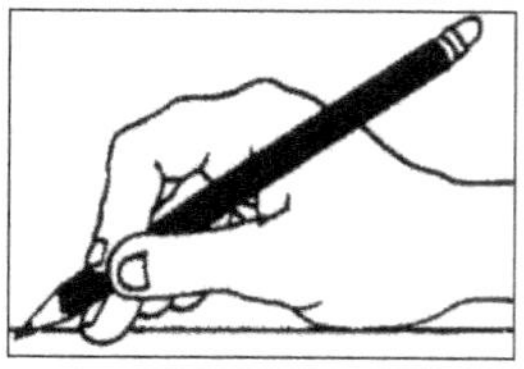

Students need to be taught the correct way to grip a pencil so they can have optimal control over the pencil point. A *tripod* grip can support this where the index finger and thumb hold the pencil against the middle finger. Students with a poor pencil grasp may benefit from using tools such as a pencil grip.

Letter Formation: Teaching Writing Strokes

Printing letters (*manuscript*) is a developmentally appropriate first step for handwriting instruction in kindergarten through grade 2. Letters can be grouped based on size and alignment. There are short letters (*a, c, e, i, m, n, o, r, s, u, v, w, x, z*), tall letters (*b, d, f, h, k, l, t*), and letters that extend below the line (*g, j, p, q, y*). Students should be taught a consistent way to form a given letter every time they write it, and then practice forming that letter many times to develop automatic and fluent handwriting skills.

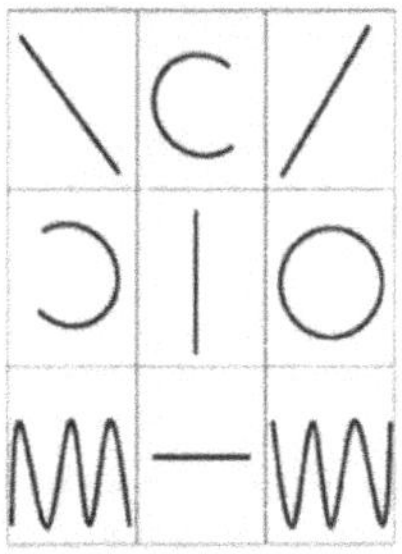

Letters are produced by a series of strokes that form curved and straight lines in different directions that are linked together. A stroke-based approach builds motor memory for the different combinations of strokes that are used to write letters. While some letters (e.g., *f, t*) require students to lift the pencil from the paper to make a second stroke, it is best to teach letter formation using a continuous stroke. Continuous stroke printing improves legibility, reduces letter reversals and directionality confusion, and increases the speed and flow of printing. Here are two examples:

- **b**: Start at the top with a vertical stroke, then make the loop to the right without lifting the pencil rather than form the line and the loop in separate strokes.

- **m**: Start at the top and draw the line down, then trace back up to start the first curve, then trace back up the first curve to make the second curve.

Students benefit from explicit instruction in how to form letters. This includes the teacher modeling by verbally explaining how to form a letter. Rhymes or songs can be used to help students remember the steps to form letters.

Students also benefit from lots of practice writing letters. Brief practice sessions are more effective than longer, periodic sessions. In the early grades, daily practice of 5-10 minutes per day is recommended. Students may need multiple opportunities (at least 5-10 times) to practice a letter using a variety of different practice formats such as copying and tracing on paper, or by tracing letters in something that gives tactile reinforcement (e.g., sand, rice, shaving cream). (Coker & Ritchey, 2015)

In kindergarten, provide lots of practice for drawing straight and curved lines that are connected together to form different pictures and designs with shapes, such as the examples in Figure 1-11. This will build coordination and graphic abilities to write letters.

Figure 1-11

Source: Skills for Action

<u>*Letter Formation During Instruction for Letter Naming and Sound-Letter Correspondence*</u>

Research has demonstrated a correlation between letter-naming and letter-writing fluency (Reutzel et. al., 2017). Handwriting should be integrated with beginning phonics instruction. As students learn to write the features of letters, they also learn to recognize them more fluently. Students should be taught how to form the uppercase and lowercase of a letter as they learn each letter. Practice with letter formation should be combined with learning sound-letter correspondences. As students write a letter, have them name it and say its sound.

One multisensory technique for reinforcing the learning of letter shapes along with sound is *sky writing*. This technique is a part of the *Orton Gillingham* approach and has been incorporated in some fashion in numerous phonics programs (Academy of Orton Gillingham). Sky writing uses the large muscles of the arm and shoulder. Students hold their arm straight in front of their chest, and with two fingers point to the sky. They then "write" the letter with their arm in the air while saying the letter and associated sound. This is repeated three times.

Instructional Suggestions:

- Encourage students to begin all uppercase letters from the top and lowercase letters from the middle or top.

- Practice letters in groups that have similar shapes so students have practice reinforcing the same motor pattern. Examples:

  - straight-line letters: *i, l, t*
  - letters that start with a small *c* shape: *a, c, d, g, o, q, s*
  - letters that start with a straight line down and then come back up and over to form a bump: b, *h, m, n, p, r*
  - diagonal letters (more difficult to form): *k, v, w, x, y, z*

- Spiral back each day to review previously taught letters.

- At first, focus on having students learn the correct motor movement to form a word. Focus attention on legibility once there is motor memory.

- Always provide visual guidance for what a letter should look like and use visual aids such as arrow cues for stroke direction and dotted letters for tracing.

Legibility

The following elements affect legibility: letter formation, letter spacing, letter alignment, letter size, word spacing. Teachers should provide specific feedback to students about how they can improve the legibility of their writing. To support letter formation and size, provide specially lined paper. For each line of print, there is a horizontal, dotted line in the middle. Short letters are written below the dotted line and above the bottom line. Tall letters are written between the top and bottom lines. The letters *g, j, p, q, y* extend below the bottom line.

For problems with word spacing, students can be taught to use a space between words by placing a popsicle stick or a finger after one word before starting another.

Handwriting Instruction Checklist

Graham and Harris (2002) developed a checklist of research-based best practices for teaching handwriting to students in the primary grades, shown in Figure 1-12.

Figure 1-12

Checklist of Best Practices

I teach children how to write each letter by:

- Showing them how it is formed.
- Describing how it is similar to and different from other letters.
- Providing practice tracing, copying, and writing the letter from memory.
- Keeping instructional sessions short, with frequent reviews and practice.
- Asking them to identify or circle their best-formed letters.
- Encouraging them to correct or rewrite poorly formed letters.
- Monitoring their practice to ensure that letters are formed correctly.
- Reinforcing their successful efforts and providing corrective feedback as needed.

I help children become more fluent in handwriting by:

- Providing them with plenty of opportunities to write.
- Eliminating interfering habits that may reduce handwriting fluency.
- Having them copy a short passage several times, trying to write it a little faster each time.

I promote handwriting development by:

- Making sure that each child develops a comfortable and efficient pencil grip.
- Encouraging children to sit in an upright position, leaning slightly forward, as they write.
- Showing them how to place or position their paper when writing.
- Teaching children to identify and name the letters of the alphabet.
- Teaching them how to write both uppercase and lowercase letters.
- Providing children with plenty of opportunities to use different types of writing instruments and paper.
- Asking children to set goals for improving specific aspects of their handwriting.
- Implementing appropriate procedures for left-handed writers, such as how to properly place or position their paper when writing.
- Monitoring students' handwriting, paying special attention to their instructional needs in letter formation, spacing, slant, alignment, size, and line quality.
- Dramatizing children's progress in handwriting through the use of charts or graphs, praise, or posting neatly written papers.

I assist students who are experiencing difficulty by:

- Organizing my class so that I can provide additional handwriting instruction to children who need it.
- Coordinating my handwriting instruction with the efforts of other professionals, such as an occupational therapist.
- Placing special emphasis on teaching difficult letters, such as *a, j, k, n, q, u,* and *z.*
- Ensuring that they master one style of handwriting before a second style is introduced.
- Considering if an alternative to handwriting, such as word processing or using a speech recognition program, is warranted.
- Helping them develop positive attitudes about handwriting.
- Talking with their parents about my handwriting program and soliciting advice.

I make sure that I:

- Encourage students to make all final drafts of papers neat and legible.
- Maintain a balanced perspective on the role of handwriting in learning to write.

Source: Graham and Harris, 2002

Cursive Handwriting, Keyboarding

There is considerable disagreement among teachers about the kind of script that students should be taught. Graham (2009-2010) notes that in the United States, children are typically taught both manuscript (print) and cursive, with manuscript taught in kindergarten through grade 2 and cursive introduced in grade 3. He also notes that research does not provide a definitive answer on the relative effectiveness of scripts, but suggests that instruction should start with manuscript in the primary grades.

Most students do not have sufficient eye-hand motor coordination to learn keyboarding to write until around grade 4. Common Core writing standard #6 first mentions keyboarding to produce writing in grade 3:

> "With guidance and support from adults, use technology to produce and publish writing (using keyboarding skills) as well as to interact and collaborate with others."

However, this standard does expect students in kindergarten through grade 2 to use digital tools to produce and publish writing with guidance and support from adults. This includes introducing them to word processing skills and features that require learning how to use a keyboard, such as dragging and dropping, and cutting and pasting.

Suggested Analysis of Spelling Errors

- **Pool:** *pll* shows that the student has some phonemic awareness and is representing beginning and ending sounds, but leaves out the medial vowel.
- **At:** *it* for *at* shows good phonemic awareness, but the student is not sure which vowel represents the short a sound.
- **Freckle:** The student is representing the first, middle, and ending sounds, but does not represent the r sound or the vowel. There is some phonemic awareness.
- **Bunch:** The student is representing the first, a middle, and an end sound, but leaves off the vowel. The use of s for ch shows that the student can hear the digraph but does not know how to spell it.
- **Drag:** At first it may seem that the student has not learned sound-letter correspondence for /d/, but because the it is followed by an r, it "sounds" like there might be a /j/ sound, which the student represents with the letter j. Phonemic awareness is better than it might appear at first.
- **You're:** This is a high frequency word that also has a contraction. Even though it is not spelled correctly, the student appears to have phonemic awareness because all the sounds are represented. Note that the letter u is used to represent the /y/ sound – the name of this letter starts with the /y/ sound.
- **Wishing:** The student represents the first consonant sound and two of the vowel sounds, but leaves off the middle consonant sound. Also, depending on how the word is pronounced and the local dialect, /ing/ may sound like /en/, which the student has represented in the spelling.
- **Black:** The student has written random letters --- there is no apparent phonemic awareness or knowledge of letter- sound correspondences.
- **Fastest:** The student has some phonemic awareness and has represented the first consonant and a few of the other consonants; the student is not sure of how to write the letter s.
- **Quiet:** At first it might seem that the student is just guessing, but when the word is pronounced, the first two sounds are /k/ and /w/ which the student has represented with the letters c and w. The final consonant sound is represented, but not the medial vowels.
- **Preacher:** The student represents the first consonant sound, has used a vowel in the middle, and ends with a final consonant sound. A mark is included above the vowel, indicating that the teacher is probably teaching short and long vowels, although it is the incorrect mark.
- **Clapping:** The student is only representing the first sound.
- **The sentence:** The student has provided one word for each spoken word in the sentence, but is clearly guessing and just using words that have already been learned such as the student's name, *no* and *mom*. The students does know how to write the basic sight word *I*.

Two-Column Take Away: Connect to the Classroom

Add notes in the right column about instructional practices you learned in this chapter.

Writing: Integration of Multiple Skills	
Research -Based Instruction	

Writing Standards Transcription Skills	

Chapter 2
Writing Community

What is meant by a community of writers? When students feel connected to each other and the teacher, they feel safe participating in writing activities. Establishing a supportive environment with opportunities for students to collaborate and give and receive feedback fosters a community of motivated writers. Publishing (showing, sharing) their work helps students feel valued in the community.

One of the four recommendations in the Institute of Education Sciences report is *Create an Engaged Community of Writers*, explains it this way (Graham et al., 2012):

> "Students need both the skill and the will to develop as writers. Teachers should establish a supportive environment in their classroom to foster a community of writers who are motivated to write well. Students and teachers also should have regular and structured opportunities to interact through giving and receiving feedback as well as collaborating on writing activities. Collaboration can increase a sense of community in a classroom. When students feel connected to one another and to the teacher, they may feel safe participating in the writing process and sharing their writing with peers." (p. 34)

Related Standards

As students engage with one another and with the teacher during shared writing experiences, as they collaborate at different stages of the writing process, and as they participate in writing conferences, they are building speaking and listening skills. The skills that are addressed in this chapter are aligned with several Common Core Speaking and Listening Standards. Grade-specific standards are provided in Figure 2-1.

Figure 2-1

#1 **Collaborative Conversation** *Prepare for and participate effectively in a range of conversations and collaborations with diverse partners, building on others' ideas and*	**Kindergarten** Participate in collaborative conversations with diverse partners about kindergarten topics and texts with peers and adults in small and larger groups. **a.** Follow agreed-upon rules for discussions (e.g., listening to others and taking turns speaking about the topics and texts under discussion). **b.** Continue a conversation through multiple exchanges.
	Grade 1 Participate in collaborative conversations with diverse partners about grade 1 topics and texts with peers and adults in small and larger groups.

expressing their own clearly and persuasively	**a.** Follow agreed-upon rules for discussions (e.g., listening to others with care, speaking one at a time about the topics and texts under discussion). **b.** Build on others' talk in conversations by responding to the comments of others through multiple exchanges. **c.** Ask questions to clear up any confusion about the topics and texts under discussion.
	Grade 2 Participate in collaborative conversations with diverse partners about grade 2 topics and texts with peers and adults in small and larger groups. **a.** Follow agreed-upon rules for discussions (e.g., gaining the floor in respectful ways, listening to others with care, speaking one at a time about the topics and texts under discussion). **b.** Build on others' talk in conversations by linking their comments to the remarks of others. **c.** Ask for clarification and further explanation as needed about the topics and texts under discussion.
#3 **Speaker's Point of View** *Evaluate a speaker's point of view, reasoning and use of evidence and rhetoric*	**Kindergarten** Ask and answer questions in order to seek help, get information, or clarify something that is not understood.
	Grade 1 Ask and answer questions about what a speaker says in order to gather additional information or clarify something that is not understood.
	Grade 2 Ask and answer questions about what a speaker says in order to clarify comprehension, gather additional information, or deepen understanding of a topic or issue.
#4 **Presenting** *Presenting information, findings, and supporting evidence such that listeners can follow the line of reasoning and the organization, development, and style are appropriate to task, purpose, and audience.*	**Kindergarten** Describe familiar people, places, things and events and with prompting and support, provide additional detail.
	Grade 1 Describe familiar people, places, things and events with relevant details expressing ideas and feelings clearly.
	Grade 2 Tell a story or recount an experience with appropriate facts and relevant, descriptive details, speaking audibly in coherent sentences.

Writing Environment

Research finds that students are more likely to learn, enjoy, and apply writing if teachers establish a supportive and motivating environment for writing. Graham, Harris, & Santangelo (2015) generated the recommendations in Figure 2-2 related to the writing environment based on their research meta-analysis.

Figure 2-2

Establish Writing Routines
That Create a Pleasant and Motivating Writing Environment

The following teaching practices and routines were found to be helpful:

1. Establish a stimulating mood during writing time and make it clear that the teacher enjoys writing and teaching it.
2. Make students' writing visible by having them share it with others, displaying it on the wall, and publishing it.
3. Create a positive classroom where students are encouraged to try hard, believe that writing skills and strategies they learn help them to write well, and attribute success to effort and the tactics they are learning.
4. Develop classroom routines, such as sharing writing in progress and completed papers with peers.
5. Set high but realistic expectations for students' writing, encouraging them to exceed previous efforts and accomplishments.
6. Adapt writing assignments and instruction so they are appropriate to students' interests and needs.
7. Keep students engaged by involving them in thoughtful (e.g., discussing ideas for writing) versus less thoughtful activities (e.g., completing a worksheet).
8. Encourage students to act in self-regulated fashion, doing as much as they can on their own.

Access to Writing Materials

A successful writing environment includes an area in the classroom that makes materials for writing accessible and well-stocked. Provide a variety of:

- Paper: unlined and lined paper, large chart paper, construction paper, journals, blank "books" (multiple pages stapled together), blank greeting cards and post cards
- Writing utensils: pencils, thin and thick markers, gel pens, coloring tools

- Additional materials: scissors, glue, tape, erasers, ink pads and stamps, paper clips, stapler, folders

Bring Writing into Learning Centers

Opportunities to write can be integrated into all areas of the classroom, including learning centers. A literacy learning center is a physical area designed for specific learning purposes that might be related to reading, writing, or speaking and listening skills. A writing center allows for targeted practice for students of skills, strategies, or techniques that have already been taught, and should be designed to provide the appropriate materials that students need to work independently or collaboratively with partners or in small groups. A specific writing center can be temporary or permanent. Examples:

Have students:

- write labels for items or places in the classroom (e.g., block area, coat closet)
- create signs – pretend road and street signs, store signs, directional signs
- write maps for places in the classroom, school, or home
- write lists – class rules and procedures, names, favorite books

Examples of classroom dramatic play areas that can include writing:

- Post Office: letters, postcards, bills
- Supermarket: grocery lists, food aisle signs
- Kitchen: menus, recipes, lists of food and cooking utensils
- Veterinary Office: lists of animals, prescriptions for pet care, directions for feeding

Teachers as Writers

In a community of writers, teachers participate as writers, not just as instructors. By taking part in writing lessons and activities, teachers convey the message that writing is important, valued, and rewarding. The Institute of Education Sciences report (Graham, et al., 2012) explains it this way:

> "Teachers should model how the ability to write affects their daily lives, demonstrate the importance of writing to communicate, model the perseverance required to create a good piece of writing, and express the satisfaction that can come from creating a meaningful text.
>
> For example, a teacher could draft a letter or email to a friend in front of students, thinking out loud to make the invisible act of composing – which occurs internally for experienced writers – more visible to students.
>
> A teacher also could collaborate with all students on a writing project, such as composing a how-to guide for carving a Halloween pumpkin or writing a class newsletter.
>
> Teachers also should take part in writing tasks. For instance, if students are asked to describe a favorite family tradition, the teacher could offer his or her own example, actively conveying how selecting a topic one is interested in can generate excitement about writing." (p. 35)

Coker (2007) makes these points about teachers as writers:

> "Children need to be introduced to the various ways in which we use writing to communicate in society and to gain practice using writing as a form of communication. An important instructional goal for developing writers is to learn that writing is similar to speaking because both offer ways to communicate with others. They benefit from opportunities to see how adults use writing and to practice those forms." (p. 104)

Before asking students to try a new writing skill or technique, it is helpful for the teacher to model how to apply it with students. This includes thinking aloud to model how to apply a skill or technique, including problem solving while writing.

Teachers should take the time to share with students all the ways they use writing in a day. Teachers can show examples of their own writing, including planning tools used and early drafts that have been revised. It helps students to see that even adult, good writers struggle to write and revise.

Interactive Writing Lesson

Interactive writing is a dynamic instructional method where the teacher and students work together following the stages of the writing process to generate a piece of text. Roth and Dabrowski (2014) explain interactive writing this way:

> In a short lesson each day, students gather as a class alongside their expert writer (the teacher) to craft and write text in a variety of genres. The "interactive" piece involves both group collaboration in composing the writing through guided conversation and a unique "sharing the pen" technique where students do the actual writing. During interactive writing, there are frequent opportunities to differentiate instruction to meet individual student needs. For example, the teacher selectively chooses how each student will participate in the lesson and negotiates the key teaching points based on the instructional value for students at that given point in time.

They recommend a writing routine that includes the components described in Figure 2-3.

Figure 2-3

Interactive Writing Lesson

Prewrite	• The teacher determines the topic for the writing piece based on a shared classroom experience, such as a read aloud book or content studied in science or social studies. • The teacher and students identify the task, audience, and purpose of the writing.

Compose, Share the Pen	• The teacher and students discuss the content of the writing. Students share their ideas as the teacher provides support by synthesizing the ideas, proposing vocabulary, and modeling sentence writing. • Teachers have the option of inviting students to take turns writing some of the text. Students might contribute letters, words, or punctuation. • The teacher uses think aloud to model specific writing skills such as spelling, spacing, or punctuation. • Editing of conventions is done either at point of error or at the end.
Review	• After the text is written, the teacher revisits a few of the writing skills or techniques emphasized while composing. This provides the opportunity of having a text in which all students have ownership to reinforce key writing principles that the students will use in their own writing.
Extend	• The class continues to use the completed writing piece as an instructional tool, including posting the piece in the classroom for students to reread, sharing the piece outside the classroom, or illustrating the piece. • The teacher might ask students to write a similar piece on their own.

The Oral Language and Literacy Connection

"Reading and writing float on a sea of talk." *James Britton, 1970*

As this quote suggests, language skills and literacy achievement are highly correlated. Research consistently demonstrates that the more children know about language, the better equipped they are to succeed in reading and writing (Burns et al., 1999; Mehta et al., 2005; Pennington et al., 2019). The National Early Literacy Panel (Lonigan & Shanahan, 2008) found that oral language – the ability to produce or comprehend spoken language – is correlated with later school achievement.

The language children are exposed to at home and in school influences the development of their language comprehension, which in turn influences their vocabulary development, development of background knowledge, comprehension skills, understanding of text structure, and ability to learn writing skills. Effective literacy instruction in the primary grades must include teaching that fosters language development, especially for students who enter kindergarten with limited exposure to language. In addition, supporting the development of language skills is essential for all students who are learning English as a second language (Calderon, 2011).

Related State Literacy Standards
There are three Common Core State Standards that are particularly related to the connection between oral language and writing. Grade-specific details for these anchor standards are included in the Appendix:

Language Anchor Standard #3

> *Apply knowledge of language to understand how language functions in different contexts, to make effective choices for meaning or style, and to comprehend more fully when reading or listening.*

Language Anchor Standard #6

> *Acquire and use accurately a range of general academic and domain-specific words and phrases sufficient for reading, writing, speaking, and listening at the college and career readiness level; demonstrate independence in gathering vocabulary.*

Speaking and Listening Anchor Standard #4

> *Presenting information, findings, and supporting evidence such that listeners can follow the line of reasoning and the organization, development, and style are appropriate to task, purpose, and audience.*

The standards make these points about the importance of oral language in developing literacy skills:

> "If literacy levels are to improve, the aims of the English language arts classroom, especially in the earliest grades, must include oral language in a purposeful, systematic way, in part because it helps students master the printed word. Besides having intrinsic value as modes of communication, listening and speaking are necessary prerequisites of reading and writing.
>
> Oral language development precedes and is the foundation for written language development; in other words, oral language is primary and written language builds on it. Children's oral language competence is strongly predictive of their facility in learning to read and write: listening and speaking vocabulary and even mastery of syntax set boundaries as to what children can read and understand no matter how well they can decode." Common Core, Appendix A, p. 26

Develop Oral Language as a Foundation for Writing

Coker and Ritchey (2015) note the following based on writing development research:

> "Writing is a social activity and writing instruction should be embedded into social contexts. Through face-to-face interactions, children come to understand that writing serves many functions, that relationships exist between speaking and writing, and that writing is aimed at, and therefore must be sensitive to, an audience." (p. 15)

It is important that teachers encourage a "productive hum" in the classroom – the sound of students talking to one another throughout the writing process, especially as they orally rehearse prior to drawing and writing.

Semantics (word meanings and relationships), *syntax* (awareness of sentence structure), and *discourse* (combining sentences to communicate ideas) are the levels of language most connected to oral or written composing. The speaking and listening vocabulary, syntactic awareness, and discourse skills that students bring to kindergarten will often depend on how much exposure to oral language they have had prior to entering school. Teachers can incorporate activities designed to grow students' oral language base that are an essential foundation for writing by creating a language-rich, language-centered classroom environment that includes:

- Teaching students how to listen and participate in conversation
- Providing opportunities for students to have extended discussions with others
- Using and modeling academic language
- Using read aloud to develop oral language skills

Teachers should do a combination of language *build-up* and *break-down* (Haynes & Maxwell). For build-up, the teacher uses more complex vocabulary, sentence structure and discourse to increase comprehension, expression, and understanding of higher order concepts. For break-down, the teacher simplifies language when children do not understand so they can improve language comprehension and understanding of concepts, and use new language to talk about new concepts.

Daily Opportunities to Write

"If you want to be a writer, you must do two things above all others: read a lot and write a lot." — Stephen King

As Stephen King, the prolific contemporary writer of suspense and science fiction notes, the best way to become better at writing is to read and write a lot. In fact, practice is the key to getting better at just about anything we want to learn – how to ski, how to play a musical instrument, how to cook. However, it is not easy to keep practicing something difficult. That is why students to whom writing comes naturally tend to want to write, and students who struggle with writing do not.

Providing daily opportunities to write is the first of four recommendations in the Institute of Education Science report (Graham et al., 2012). It is important for teachers to provide time for dedicated writing instruction and writing for a variety of purposes during science, social studies, math, art, and other subjects. The report suggests the following:

> "Providing adequate time for students to write is one essential element of an effective writing instruction program. However, recent surveys of elementary teachers indicate that students spend little time writing during the school day. Students need dedicated instructional time to learn the skills and strategies necessary to become effective writers, as well as time to practice what they learn. Time for writing practice can help students gain confidence in their writing abilities.

> The panel recommends a **minimum of one hour a day** devoted to writing for students beginning in first grade. The hour should include at least 30 minutes dedicated to teaching a variety of writing strategies, techniques, and skills appropriate to students' levels. The remaining 30 minutes should be spent on writing practice, where students apply the skills they learned from writing-skills instruction. For children in kindergarten, at least 30 min each day should be devoted to writing and developing writing skills." (p. 10-11)

Types of Writing Tasks

Beginning in grade 3, Common Core writing standard #10 expects students to "Write routinely over extended time frames (time for research, reflection, and revision) and shorter time frames (a single sitting or a day or two) for a range of discipline-specific tasks, purposes, and audiences." Keeping this in mind, the types of writing tasks that teachers ask primary grade students to complete can be organized into two categories, as detailed in Figure 2-4.

Figure 2-4

Shorter Writing Tasks	Extended Writing Tasks
- completed in less than 10 minutes - informal Examples: - drawing (K-1) - labeling - phrase or sentence writing - spelling or handwriting practice	- completed in one or more lessons - informal or formal Examples: - drawing and dictating (K-1) - sentence, paragraph writing - response to narrative text - writing from sources

Writing Throughout the School Day

In order to find enough time for students to get sufficient writing practice, teachers must embed writing throughout the day. The Institute for Education Science report offers this suggestion:

> "Time for writing practice can occur in the context of other content-area instruction. Additionally, students can write before, during, and/or after reading to articulate what they already know, what they want to know, and what they learned. When teachers integrate writing tasks with other content-area lessons, students may think more critically about the content-area material." (Graham et al., 2012, p. 11)

When we teach students science, social studies, and math concepts and ask them to write about what they have learned, it helps to solidify their learning. For example:

- When studying the life cycle of plants in first grade, students might be asked to write a sentence about the importance of roots to a plant.

- As part of social studies in second grade, students might write a paragraph about the process immigrants went through when arriving at Ellis Island.

When students write about content, teachers should ask them to incorporate the related new content vocabulary. Remember that students must have at least a basic understanding about a topic before they can write something about it.

Response Journals: Responding to Narrative Text
One of the research-based recommendations in the *Writing to Read* report (Graham & Hebert, 2010) is to have students write a personal response to narrative text. Personal responses to text help students clarify and organize what they are reading and become aware of their reactions to the text. It is helpful to let students know that there is no "right" or "wrong" response because they are writing about their personal response.

Responding to narrative text might take the form of a response journal where the teacher asks students to draw or write their feelings, reactions, and questions during or after reading (or listening to) a story or other form of narrative text such as a biography. The teacher (or another adult) might review the students' comments and then write a response back to the student in the journal, such as a comment or question.

Guiding Questions for Response Journals

Figure 2-5 lists questions that teachers might provide to guide students as they consider what they want to say about a piece of narrative text. It is best to ask just one or two questions, or ask students to select one or two from a short list of questions.

Figure 2-5

Overall Personal Response

- What did you feel as you were reading (or listening to the read aloud)?
- Is there something that reminds you of yourself or people you know?
- Is there something that reminds you of something that happened in your life?
- Is there a confusing passage or part of the story?
- What do you agree or disagree with?
- What do you like or dislike most about the story?
- Is there something you wonder about in the story?
- Is there something you wish had happened differently?
- Is there something that surprised you in the story?
- What is your overall opinion of this story? Would you recommend it to a friend?
- Does this story remind you of another story you have read?

Response to Theme

- What do you think is important in the story?
- Is there a lesson to be learned in the story?

Response to Characters

- What is your opinion of the characters?
- Did the main character change throughout the story?
- What was the main character's problem, and how did they solve that problem?
- Do you agree with the actions of the characters? Would your actions be similar or different?

Response to Setting

- What is your reaction to the setting(s) in the story (including time and place)?
- How does the setting fit into the story, and why is it important?

Response to the Author

- Why do you think the author wrote this story?
- What do you think about the author's choice for the title?
- Does the author make you feel that you are part of the story? How does the author do this?
- What did you like about the author's writing?
- Did you learn something you might try in your writing?

Give Students Choice

Most people appreciate having choice, and the same is true for students. Glover (2014) notes that when students are able to choose a writing topic, they are more motivated to write, have more stamina because they are writing about a topic they care about, and are better able to develop an image of themselves as having ideas that are worth writing about. Over time, when given choices, students are more willing to take risks with their writing and to share their work.

Giving students writing choices is a recommendation in the Institute of Education Sciences report (Graham et al., 2012):

> "Teachers should provide opportunities for student choice in writing assignments— for example, choice in selecting writing topics or the freedom to modify a teacher-selected prompt. Teachers also can encourage students to write for themselves; their peers; an imaginary audience (e.g., a character in a story); adults (e.g., their parents or an author); or a wider, unknown audience." (p. 36)

Here are some suggestions for activities that foster choice:

- <u>Writing Topic Notebook:</u> Students keep a notebook in which they record topics for writing, such as memories, pets, vacations, "firsts" (e.g., the first time riding a bike, first soccer goal, first day at camp), and favorite holidays. Students can add topics often and consult their notebooks throughout the school year. Teachers can model how to use a notebook by keeping their own topic notebook.

- <u>Weekly Class Newsletter:</u> The teacher generates a class newsletter highlighting events from the week. Students choose the topic for the entry they contribute to the newsletter.

- Weekly Class Blog with Guest Writers: This is an electronic option, similar to the newsletter. Administrators, teachers, parents, and students are invited to follow the blog during the school year. Over the course of the year, each student has the opportunity to be a "guest blogger", focusing on a highlight of the week. The "audience" is encouraged to leave responses on the blog.

Choice Within Topics Provided by the Teacher

Giving students some choice does not mean that teachers must leave it completely up to students to decide what they will write about. Teachers can provide a choice within an assigned topic. This is helpful because:

- Some students who have limited language skills may feel stress because they do not know what to write about.
- Many students benefit from having prompts to stimulate ideas before they write.
- Teacher-generated topics give students experience with different kinds of writing tasks related to different content areas.

Choice related to Visual Prompts

Illustrations and pictures are excellent "springboards" for writing. For example:

- Show a picture from a read aloud book and ask students to write about the main character, setting, or event.
- Show a picture related to the science or social studies topic you are teaching and ask students to write what they know about that topic.
- Show an unusual picture and ask students to write a creative story or explanation related to the picture. Use *who, what, where, why,* and *when* questions as a scaffold to help students generate writing ideas.

More Ideas for Choice Within a Topic

Figure 2-6 lists suggestions for writing topics that are organized into the three types of writing. Students can be given a choice within these topics.

Figure 2-6

Suggestions for Choice Within Topics

Informational Writing
• Describe something in this picture • Describe something about this person/place • Give directions to a place of your choosing • Give directions to make something of your choosing • Explain a wish you have related to something of your choosing • Explain how something works • Compare and contrast any two of the following • Write about what lives in one of the following places • Make a list of the people from one of these categories • Make a list of different things that people collect
Opinion Writing
• I like/prefer this kind of candy/animal/game • I like this book/movie/television show • My favorite color/song/season/holiday is • The character I like most is • My favorite part of this ____ is • A special treasure to me is
Narrative Writing
• Create a story from this picture • Imagine what would happen if • Rewrite the ending of this story • List the big events from the life of one of these people • Tell what happened in one of these fables • Explain what happened in one of these videos • Describe the main character's problem in one of these stories • Share a time when you were happy/sad/confused/ embarrassed/proud • Pick any day and tell what happened to you on that day

Authentic Writing Tasks

Whenever possible, teachers should assign *authentic* writing tasks where students are writing to real audiences with real reasons for writing. This type of writing provides opportunities for students to see how writing is used outside of the classroom as a means to communicate for a specific purpose. These kinds of tasks help students realize their voice can be heard through writing.

Assigning writing for a real purpose and audience is an instructional practice that has been found to motivate and engage students across all grades (Hidi & Boscolo, 2006; Boscolo & Gelati, 2007). Many older students conclude that the only audience for their writing is their teachers. If students learn at an early age that writing can be used to communicate their ideas in the real world, they will more likely be motivated to write in the upper grades.

Anne Rodier of the National Writing Project (2000) makes this point about authentic audiences:

> "Students have to believe that what they have to say is important enough to bother writing. They have to have the experience of writing for real audiences before they will know that writing can bring them power."

Teachers can assign writing tasks that demonstrate the importance of using writing to communicate with others or as a tool for remembering. Examples of authentic audiences include members of the school community, younger or older students, family members, peers or pen pals, and published authors. Figure 2-7 lists examples of authentic writing tasks.

Figure 2-7

Examples of Authentic Writing Tasks

- plans for building a dog house
- writing a list of groceries
- thank you note after a field trip
- directions for making a peanut butter and jelly sandwich
- list for Santa
- book or movie review
- shared journal entries with another student

Writing tasks in imaginative play centers:

- classroom post office where students can mail notes to each other and others outside the classroom
- mock restaurant where students write menus and take orders
- mock veterinary office where doctors record the condition of imaginary animals who are treated
- classroom newsroom where students write stories for online or print classroom newsletters

Writing Block: Writing Lesson Routine

During the time formally dedicated to teaching and practicing writing (typically called a *writing block*), teachers should follow a consistent lesson format. The *Keys to Early Writing* lesson routine in Figure 2-8 offers a structure that incorporates research-based instructional suggestions. Keep in mind that instruction time for teaching spelling should occur during time designated to teaching phonics and word study skills. Time for specific practice of handwriting should also take place outside this lesson routine. A template for planning a writing lesson based on this format is included at the end of this chapter. The writing block should be between 35 and 55 minutes long. The suggested approximate time spent on each stage is 35% for *Launch,* 50% for *Explore*, and 15% for *Land.*

Figure 2-8

Writing Lesson Routine

LAUNCH *15-20 minutes*	• Teacher explicitly teaches or reviews writing skills or techniques – Uses modeling and think aloud – Shares mentor text (published or by teacher/student) • Format: Usually whole group
EXPLORE *15-25 minutes*	• Students practice application of writing skills or techniques with a new or continuing writing task – Teacher provides differentiated guided practice – Includes teacher or peer conferencing • Format: Independent, partner, and small group
LAND *5-10 minutes*	• Teachers and students reflect on what was learned – Sharing and public celebration of student writing – Giving and receiving feedback – Revision of writing as needed • Format: Whole or small group

More About the LAUNCH Stage

Research finds that students benefit from explicit and direct instruction for skills that are used throughout the writing process, following a gradual release of responsibility model (Graham et al., 2012). Over time, students develop a repertoire of writing skills that they can apply when writing. During this stage of the writing lesson, teachers introduce or continue to review a writing skill or technique by explaining its purpose and how it can be used. Teachers model its use before having students practice with peers or work independently.

Showing mentor text that provides examples of the writing skill or technique enables students to emulate it in their own writing. Teachers can show several examples and provide time for students to discuss how the author applied the skill or technique.

The number of lessons that are devoted to each skill or technique will vary, with some requiring multiple lessons before students can use them in their own writing. The focus for a set of lessons should be determined as part of a broader plan for the school year that identifies a series of teaching units that address major writing topics. Decisions about the topics and the order for teaching these units will vary depending on the needs of the students and the demands of the writing curriculum being used in the school. Here are some suggestions of topics for teaching units that are aligned with the *Keys to Early Writing* instructional framework:

- How to participate in a writing community
- Drawing
- Labeling, writing lists
- Stages of the writing process
- How to generate ideas for writing
- Telling more, adding details
- Sentence skills: sentence types and punctuation, sentence combining, sentence elaboration
- Paragraph writing
- Text structure for the three types of writing
- Using text features
- Writing introductions and conclusions
- Using patterns of organization (description, sequence, cause and effect, compare and contrast, problem and solution)
- Using transition words and phrases
- Poetry
- Writing with task, audience and purpose in mind
- Writer's craft techniques
- Skills for writing about reading and writing from sources

More About the EXPLORE Stage

This stage of the writing lesson includes time for students to independently practice using a skill or technique in their own writing. It also includes time for collaboration and feedback with the teacher and with peers.

Collaboration helps students make decisions about what to write and how to incorporate a writing skill into their own writing. Research suggests that having students work together is an effective practice. Graham, Harris, and Santangelo (2015) found that a common characteristic of successful collaborative writing was that students were provided with specific directions for what to do when working together and then taught how to carry out these guidelines. They also found that it is helpful to establish routines where students share their work with others.

Once students demonstrate an understanding of a writing skill or technique, they should practice applying it as they write independently. Research finds that writing quality is enhanced when teachers set high, but realistic expectations for students' writing, including setting clear, specific, and reasonably challenging goals (Graham, Harris & Santangelo, 2015). Teachers may need to model and provide guided practice several times before students can apply a skill independently. Graham and colleagues (2012) point out that there are differences in when students are ready to apply a skill independently:

> "Teachers should make sure they do not release responsibility to students too early. In some cases, this may mean having students spend more time in activities that are teacher directed until they develop the knowledge and skills to become more independent. Conversely, if some students are particularly strong in understanding and applying a new strategy, teachers can create collaborative peer groups in which more adept students help peers better understand, use, and apply new strategies."

More About the LAND Stage

At the LAND stage of the writing lesson, the teacher and students *land back* to where they started. The teacher wraps up the lesson by reviewing the skill or technique that was the focus during LAUNCH and the objective for the lesson. The teacher can also set the stage for the next writing lesson.

The LAND stage is also the time for students to share their writing with the community. Sharing is important because writing is a social act. We write to communicate and sharing time reinforces that as students become more aware that their peer audience is interested in seeing their writing. Options for sharing include:

- A few students are invited to share their work with the whole group. The teacher keeps track to be sure all students have an opportunity to share over time.
- Students share their work in small groups or with a partner.
- Students share a drawing, a text draft, part of a writing piece, or a completed writing piece.

Giving and receiving feedback can occur as students share their work, which can lead to revision of work at the LAND step or as part of the plan for the EXPLORE step in the next writing lesson.

Celebrating the Writer

Primary students should see and celebrate themselves as writers! Celebrating writing makes student writing more exciting and meaningful. Here are some suggestions:

- Showcase student drawings and writing pieces by posting them in the classroom and hallways. Then conduct a gallery walk where students add stickers or positive comments on sticky notes to others' writing pieces. Parents and guests can be invited to view the pieces.
- Keep adding to an anchor chart that lists elements that students want to celebrate in their own or peer writing.
- Video tape students reading or describing their work, then make the videos available for others to watch.
- Create a classroom version of a "red carpet" or "center stage" where students stand and use a pretend microphone to share all or part of their work.

- Set aside a few minutes each week for a writing celebration that recognizes the writing pieces completed that week. Use party hats, noise-makers, and other party items as part of the celebration.

Author's Chair

Author's Chair is an example of an activity teachers can use to model sample language that encourages appropriate verbal peer feedback. In this activity, students practice giving constructive comments and positive statements about peers' writing (Graham et al., 2012).

Activity directions:

During this activity, one student, sitting in a special chair, reads their work to peers as they sit on the floor. The teacher then models and facilitates giving kind, verbal comments, such as the following:

- I really like ___________.
- A standout line in your text for me is _________ because _________.
- I could really picture _________ because _________.

Writing Lesson Routine: Planning Guide

LAUNCH *15-20 minutes* 	Skill, technique: Introduce or review? Mentor text: Whole group, small group, independent work:
EXPLORE *15-25 minutes* 	What will students do? What will I do? Will there be conferencing? Whole group, small group, independent work:
LAND *5-10 minutes* 	How will students reflect on what was learned? How will students share and celebrate their work? Will there be an opportunity to give/receive feedback? Will there be an opportunity to revise? Whole group, small group, independent work:

Two-Column Take Away: Connect to the Classroom

Add notes in the right column about instructional practices you learned in this chapter.

Writing Environment, Teacher as Writer	
Oral Language Foundation	

Daily Writing Tasks, Choice Authentic Audience	

Writing Lesson Plan	

Chapter 3
The Writing Process

It is well-accepted practice that students should be taught the stages of the writing process, beginning in the elementary grades. The Common Core writing standards expect students to recognize and use the stages of the writing process by third grade, with the concept introduced in prior grades. View the grade specific details for writing standard #5 in Figure 3-1.

Figure 3-1

#5 Writing Process *Develop and strengthen writing as needed by planning, revising, editing, rewriting, or trying a new approach.*	**Kindergarten** With guidance and support from adults, respond to questions and suggestions from peers and add details to strengthen writing as needed.
	Grade 1 With guidance and support from adults, focus on a topic, respond to questions and suggestions from peers, and add details to strengthen writing as needed.
	Grade 2 With guidance and support from adults and peers, focus on a topic and strengthen writing as needed by revising and editing.
	Grade 3 With guidance and support from peers and adults, develop and strengthen writing as needed by planning, revising, and editing .

Teaching students to use the writing process for a variety of purposes is one of the recommendations in the Institute of Educations Sciences research report (Graham et al., 2012) which explains the writing process:

> "The writing process is the means through which a writer composes text. Writing is not a linear process, like following a recipe to bake a cake. It is flexible; writers should learn to move easily back and forth between components of the writing process, often alternating their plans and revising their text along the way. Components of the writing process include planning, drafting, sharing, evaluating, revising, and editing. An individual component, publishing, may be included to develop a shared final product." (p. 14)

History of the Writing Process

Beginning in the 1960s, in order to understand how to teach writing, Hayes and Flower researched the steps that successful writers follow when they write. They developed a model of the writing process with three stages: *planning, translating,* and *reviewing.* Over the years, the model was informed by new research and modified to include four stages (Hayes, 1980, 1996, 2004) as shown in Figure 3-2.

Figure 3-2

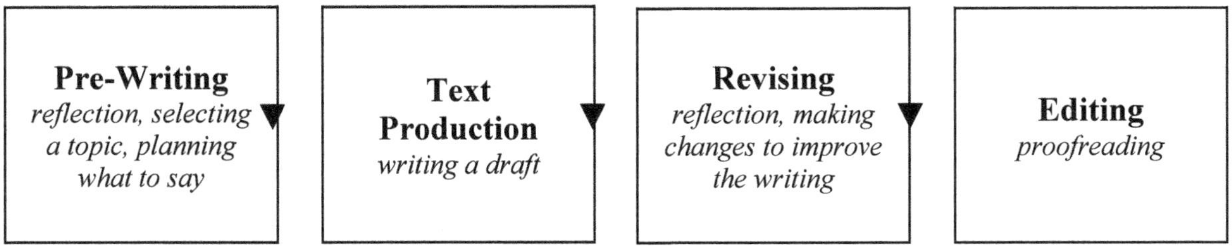

Keys to Literacy: *The Process Writing Routine*

Keys to Literacy has developed an acronym to help students in grades 3 through 12 recall the stages in the writing process (Sedita, 2013, 2015), explained in Figure 3-3. These stages have been simplified for young students in primary grades, as shown in Figure 3-4 and the anchor chart shown in Figure 3-5 that includes visual cues to remind students about each stage of the writing process. Students in kindergarten and grade 1 may not be developmentally ready to formally revise their work, and instead may focus on adding more to their drawings, labels, phrases, or sentences.

Figure 3-3

THE PROCESS WRITING ROUTINE

The first letter of each word in the title refers to the four major stages of the writing process:

Think, Plan, Write, Revise

The arrow is added to remind students that the writing process is dynamic and recursive. Writers repeat and revisit the stages several times as they develop a piece of writing.

	**Think**	• Identify the audience and purpose • Brainstorm topic/ideas • Gather information • Take notes
	Plan	• Organize ideas • Use a planning guide
	Write	• Follow the guide • Translate ideas into sentences and paragraphs
	Revise	• Reread writing • Work with peers or teacher to receive feedback • Add details to strengthen or clarify • Proofread and edit for conventions

Figure 3-4

The Process Writing Routine: Primary Grades

<table>
<tr><td rowspan="2">Think & Plan</td><td>generating ideas and organizing</td><td>Students respond to:<ul><li>What do I want to say?</li><li>How will I present what I want to say?</li></ul></td></tr>
<tr><td colspan="2">Teachers:<ul><li>State clear student objectives (product and process)</li><li>Lead brainstorm and help narrow the topic</li><li>Provide opportunities for oral rehearsal</li><li>Share planning tools</li></ul></td></tr>
<tr><td rowspan="2">Write</td><td>using drawing, words</td><td>Students respond to:<ul><li>How can I use drawings, words, and sentences to communicate what I want to say?</li></ul></td></tr>
<tr><td colspan="2">Teachers:<ul><li>Ensure that writers focus on composing, not transcription skills</li><li>Provide scaffolds as needed</li><li>Provide opportunities for shared writing</li></ul></td></tr>
<tr><td rowspan="2">Revise</td><td>improving</td><td>Students respond to:<ul><li>Can I add more detail?</li><li>How can I improve what I said?</li></ul></td></tr>
<tr><td colspan="2">Teachers:<ul><li>Focus on revising for content
– Is the message of the writer clear?</li><li>Provide opportunities for feedback
– What did the writer do well?
– What is the one thing that will make this writing stronger?</li><li>Edit for conventions
– What transcription skills need to be worked on?</li></ul></td></tr>
</table>

Figure 3-5

Think & Plan	
Write	
Revise	

Activities to Teach the Writing Process

Figures 3-6 and 3-7 present examples of classroom activities that will introduce the stages of the writing process to young students.

Figure 3-6

***Play-Doh* Activity**

This is a hands-on activity that uses at least two different colors of *Play-Doh*. Students work in pairs or groups of three.

Directions to students:

- Work with a partner(s). The task is to make something with *Play-Doh*. The audience is your classmates. The purpose is to make something that reminds us of _____ (e.g., food, animals, plants).
- (THINK & PLAN) Work with your partner to brainstorm ideas for an object you might make. Consider the audience and purpose.
- (WRITE) Work independently to build an object out of a single color of *Play-Doh.*
- Talk with a partner about what you made. Give suggestions to each other about details you might add using a different color of *Play-Doh.*
- (REVISE) Add details using the second color.
- Label your piece by adding a title and your name.

When the pieces are completed, place them around the room and allow students to have a gallery walk. Encourage them to use the terms related to the writing process as they share the steps they followed.

Figure 3-7

FIVE-DAY WRITING PROCESS

This is an example of a week-long activity that culminates in publishing writing pieces. This activity should only be used with students who are able to write a sentence.

Day 1 Think and Plan

- Brainstorm 5 topics you could write about.

Day 2 Write

- Pick one of the topics.
- Write a sentence about that topic.
- Underline the naming part, double underline the action part.

Day 3 Revise Content

- Conference: Read your sentence to a partner.
- Revise: Work with your partner to add one detail to the naming part and one detail to the action part. Use *who, where, when, why* and *how* questions as a scaffold.
- Conference: Read the sentence to two different partners; each partner initials it if it makes sense.
- Revise: If the sentence does not make sense, work with your partners to fix the sentence.

Day 4 Revise Conventions

- Conference with the teacher and edit for spelling, grammar, punctuation.

Day 5 Publishing

- Write or type the final version of the sentence neatly.
- Sign the piece.
- Post sentences around the room.

Adapted from "Write Traits: 6 Trait Instruction and Assessment"

Explicit Instruction and Scaffolds
Students benefit from explicit instruction for the specific skills and strategies they must employ at each stage of the writing process. Graham and Perin (2007) explain that explicitly and systematically teaching students strategies for planning, revising, and editing their compositions has shown a dramatic effect on the quality of students' writing, and note:

> "The ultimate goal is to teach students to use these strategies independently. Strategy instruction may involve teaching more generic processes, such as brainstorming or collaboration for peer revising. In other instances, it involves teaching strategies for accomplishing specific types of writing tasks, such as writing a story or a persuasive essay.

Whether generic or highly focused, explicitly teaching strategies for planning, revising, and/or editing has a strong impact on the quality of their writing." (pp 15-16)

Suggestions for teaching writing skills, strategies and techniques that are used at the various stages of the writing process are provided throughout the *Keys to Early Writing* chapters.

Scaffolds

Students also benefit from scaffolds that provide assistance as students are learning a writing skill. This assistance is removed once the skill is learned. Instructional scaffolds for writing include:

- Breaking a writing task into smaller, more manageable parts
- Providing word lists (with pictures), prompts, tips, questions, or cue cards
- Providing templates, graphic organizers, checklists, activity guides
- Providing opportunities for students to work collaboratively

Figure 3-8 identifies the scaffolds that are suggested in *Keys to Early Writing*, organized by stages in the writing process.

Figure 3-8

Keys to Early Writing Scaffolds

Process Stage	***Scaffold***
THINK & PLAN	• Scaffolded text sources *(annotation, read aloud)* • Top-down topic web • Two-column notes
WRITE	• Word lists *(with pictures)* • Sentence frames • Transition lists • Writing templates
REVISE	• Feedback checklists
All Stages	• Think aloud • Mentor text models • Peer and teacher collaboration • Oral rehearsal

Collaboration at All Stages of the Writing Process

As you learned in Chapter 2, writing is a social activity and collaborative arrangements in which students work together at all stages of the writing process have been identified as highly effective (Graham, Harris, & Santangelo, 2015). Figure 3-9 suggests opportunities for students to collaborate across the stages of the writing process.

Figure 3-9

Collaboration

Students can collaborate at the THINK and PLAN stages to:

- Brainstorm ideas for a topic
- Decide on an audience
- Gather information from sources
- Take notes
- Determine how to organize a drawing or writing piece
- Complete a writing guide provided by the teacher

Students can collaborate at the WRITE stage to:

- Create a drawing and add labels
- Generate words to form sentences or paragraphs
- Contribute a page for a class book
- Incorporate transition words
- Spell words correctly
- Use capitalization and punctuation correctly

Students can collaborate at the REVISE stage to:

- Provide suggestions for how to elaborate on the content of a drawing or writing piece
- Provide suggestions for how to better organize a writing piece
- Provide suggestions for how to improve sentence structure
- Help edit for spelling, capitalization, and punctuation

One way that students can collaborate is to complete an activity that has a group of students generating a single text. An example is the *Star of the Day* activity described in Figure 3-10 (Ramirez, 2006 in Graham et al., 2012).

Figure 3-10

Star of the Day

Each student is celebrated on their own day. Seated in the front of the classroom, the *Star of the Day* answers interview questions from peers using a pretend microphone. After the interview, the other students compose sentences about the *Star of the Day*. They can do this in pairs or small groups. These sentences are shared and combined into a class paragraph, which is then displayed on the class bulletin board. The paragraph should begin with this sentence: *(name) is the Star of the Day*. For grades K and 1, the students can provide oral sentences that the teacher scribes on a board or chart paper. For grade 2, the students can write out their sentences on sentence strips.

Example:

__________ is the Star of the Day. He likes the color red. He loves to eat cupcakes. His favorite animal is an elephant. ________ lives in Boston. It's his birthday today!

Another example is the creation of a *class book,* which is a compilation of pages contributed by multiple students. The teacher identifies a topic and asks students to complete their own drawing and/or text that will be included in the class book. Students can work collaboratively at the think and plan, write, or revise stages of the writing process. The whole class can produce one book, or smaller groups of students can produce books.

The topic for a class book can be related to content instruction (e.g., pages for different kinds of weather for science or countries for social studies). A class book can be a collection of personal responses (e.g., journal entries) to a narrative text. A book might also be created following a technique used in a mentor text. For example, in the book *Brown Bear, Brown Bear, What Do You See?* by Bill Martin and Eric Carle, a bear sees and names a different animal on each page. Using this book as an example, students might create a page for a class book for an animal of their choosing.

Teaching Collaboration

It takes time and deliberate effort to create a collaborative environment where the teacher and students feel comfortable sharing ideas and giving feedback. For the teacher, it may seem overwhelming to have students talking and working together in partners or groups as it may get loud and sometimes feel "out of control." Do not be discouraged! If you take the time to teach students how to collaborate, including rules for acceptable collaborative behavior, you will be able to use this strategy to support writing instruction.

Students benefit from explicit instruction for how to collaborate, including guided practice opportunities before they can be expected to work with peers independently. Teachers can use role-play to model appropriate peer discussion.

Teachers can share collaborative guidelines, such as those suggested in the chart in Figure 3-11.

Figure 3-11

What does collaboration look, sound, and feel like?	
Looks like	• Students sit near each other. • Students take turns. • Students stay focused on the task.
Sounds like	• There is a "productive hum" in the classroom from students talking. • There is conversation about writing, including students asking question of one another.
Feels like	• Supportive • Productive • Positive

Options for Assigning Partners or Small Groups

There are two options for grouping students for peer collaboration:

Teacher-assigned

- Homogeneous grouping: students with the same skill levels
- Heterogeneous grouping: students with different skill levels (students with proficient writing skills paired with students with less proficiency)

Student-choice

- Potential benefit: tends to foster more engagement
- Potential challenge: more difficult to manage

Consider personalities and potential challenges when making decisions about how to group students. Here are some general tips for grouping students:

- Plan how students will be grouped ahead of time.
- Avoid always using the same grouping – alternate your method of group selection.

- Set clear expectations for behavior, process, goals, and final product.
- Assign roles (e.g., facilitator, scribe, presenter).
- Provide interaction and communication rules (e.g., take turns talking, no interrupting, everyone participates).
- Be clear about the task to be completed and the amount of time for collaboration.

Feedback and Revision

Revision is a sequence of changes in a writing piece in which ideas, words, phrases, and sentences are added, deleted, moved, or changed. Editing is the part of revising that makes changes related to conventions (spelling, capitalization, punctuation).

Feedback

Feedback is typically provided by the teacher or peers during the EXPLORE and LAND stages of the writing lesson. Providing students with opportunities to give and receive feedback throughout the writing process is one of the recommendations in the Institute of Education Sciences report (Graham et al., 2012). The report suggests:

> "Students need to know whether their writing is accurately and appropriately conveying its message. One way students can determine this is by sharing their writing and responding to written and verbal feedback from the teacher and their peers. Although teachers should provide feedback to students through teacher-student conferences and rubrics, peers also should be encouraged to participate in the feedback process. When students provide feedback to peers, their comments and observations may enhance their understanding of their own writing. Students need to be taught strategies and appropriate language for written feedback. Teachers should also provide sample language to encourage appropriate verbal feedback." (p. 37)

Developmental Readiness for Revision

At what grade is it developmentally appropriate to expect students to participate in conferencing, collaborative feedback, and revision of their own writing? There is a significant difference between the developmental readiness of students entering kindergarten and students leaving grade 2.

Developmental readiness for revision will vary greatly for kindergarten and grade 1 students. Revision in kindergarten tends to be more about *adding on* than revising the actual content and wording of a writing piece or drawing. When students share their writing with someone else, they may realize (or the listener may suggest) that they have more they can add.

As students move into grade 2, they become better able to revise and edit sentences and paragraphs based on feedback from others and from reading their own writing.

Teacher Feedback to Support Revision

It is important to find time for students to receive feedback. The feedback that students receive matters as much as writing instruction itself. Without feedback, students cannot learn how to improve their writing. Students also need time to improve their work through revision.

Teachers should emphasize meaning over form and correctness in early drafts so students learn to review their own work and give peer feedback that focuses on more than spelling and mechanics. Here are some guidelines for effective feedback for any grade level (Bangert-Downs, et al., 1991; Walberg, 1999; Wiggins, 1993; 2012):

- Provide feedback about the final product AND throughout the process.
- Provide user-friendly feedback that is specific, concrete, and manageable. Feedback is not of much value if the student cannot understand it or is overwhelmed by it.
- Make the desired outcomes clearer by using criterion-referenced feedback (e.g., checklists, rubrics).
- The sooner feedback can be provided the better. The longer students have to wait for feedback, the weaker the connection to their effort becomes and the less likely they are to benefit.
- Provide opportunities for students to give feedback to their peers and to provide their own feedback by monitoring their work against established criteria.
- Make the feedback actionable by providing opportunities and time for students to revise their work.

Targeted Feedback

Students are less likely to become overwhelmed if teachers target their feedback, focusing on just one or two areas. Feedback should be linked back to the main objective of a writing lesson. It can be the same feedback for all students in the class, or it can be different for each student.

Examples of specific feedback topics:

- labeling or adding details to a drawing
- including space between words
- using more varied vocabulary
- turning a phrase into a complete sentence
- expanding sentences
- combining sentences
- adding or editing sentence punctuation, capitalization
- using transition words and phrases
- generating or improving an introduction or conclusion
- completing a graphic organizer
- gathering information from a source into a list or notes

Feedback Checklists

As noted above, research has identified the use of criterion-referenced tools such as checklists as effective for providing teacher and peer feedback to students across all grades. Young children in kindergarten and grade 1 typically do not have the reading ability to benefit from formal checklists. However, a simple set of questions such as those in Figure 3-12 can be used to help students consider how to improve their drawings or writing in these grades. Some students in grade 2 may be developmentally ready to use a peer feedback form such as the examples shown in Chapter 8.

Figure 3-12

My Writing

- What do I like about my writing?
- What can I do to make it better?
- What is something I learned about writing while I wrote this piece?

<u>*Glow and Grow*</u>

Glow and Grow is an activity that teachers can use to support and nurture young writers. It can be used to extend students' drawings or written text. Figure 3-13 includes directions and an example of a template that can be used.

Figure 3-13

Glow & Grow

- Peers or the teacher listen to the student explain their drawing or read aloud the writing.
- Peers or the teacher add a positive comment (GLOW).
- Through questioning, peers or the teacher guide the student to enhance their drawing or writing by adding something (GROW).

Keep the following in mind when using *Glow and Grow* with students' drawings:

- A drawing should be an accurate reflection of the student's ideas.
- Remind students that the purpose of their drawing is to convey their message to someone else, so drawings should include as many details as possible.
- The more detailed students make their pictures, the more opportunities they will have to add labels and expand their use of vocabulary.

- Ask students specific questions to expand their drawings. For example, "What color was the sun that day?" or "How many circles would you like in your snowman?"
- Encourage students to add academic words they have been learning in class (e.g., in science add the words *stem*, *root*, *bud* to their drawing about growing a plant).

Questions to Support Feedback & Revision

Question terms such as *who, when, what, why, where,* and *how* can serve as a scaffold for giving peer feedback and to help students revise their work, especially for adding more to their drawings and sentences. Question cards such as those shown in Figure 3-14 can be used as a scaffold. For example, a student might show the *Where?* card and ask a peer who has drawn a picture of a dog, "*Where* is the dog?" The student might then add something about the setting. If asked "*What* is the dog doing?" the student might show the dog eating or running. Question cards are also addressed in Chapter 6, and a set of full-size cards is included in the Appendix.

Figure 3-14

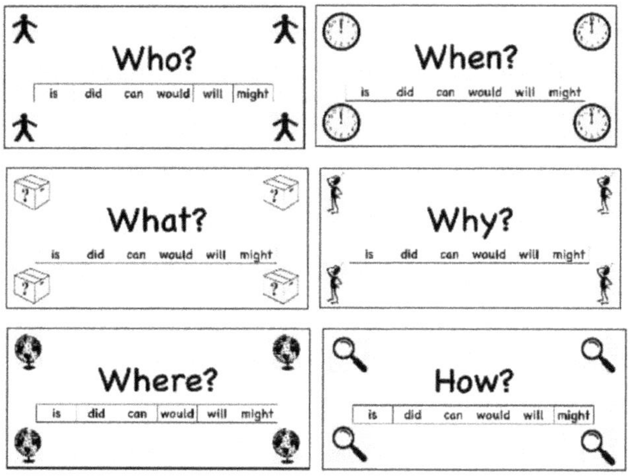

Focus Revision on Content

Unfortunately, both teachers and students tend to focus on correcting mechanics, which can be described as "surface errors". Shelbie Witte (2013) makes this suggestion:

> "Teachers need to help students realize that revising is not about just fixing grammatical and surface errors, but also refers to the strength of an opinion and overall structure of a piece, including content. A focus on form over the development of content and ideas can quickly cut off the excitement of composing."

When students focus revision on the content of their writing, they clarify and reshape their writing to effectively communicate their points. This does not mean, however, that spelling, punctuation, and grammar conventions are unimportant, only that they should be addressed separately from content revision.

ARMS and *CUPS* are two widely used acronyms that highlight the difference between revising content and editing for conventions, shown in Figure 3-15. Teachers can introduce these scaffolds to students who are developmentally ready to revise. It is helpful to post these as anchor charts in the classroom.

Figure 3-15

ARMS		CUPS	
A	Add: details, words, sentences	**C**	Capitalization: beginning of a sentence, proper names
R	Remove: words or sentences that don't make sense	**U**	Usage: match nouns and verbs
M	Move: words or sentences to fit in a better spot	**P**	Punctuation: . ? ! , " "
S	Substitute: better words	**S**	Spelling

Conferencing

A writing conference is a meeting to discuss student work. It is a time to respond, provide support, ask questions, gain understanding, and/or give feedback. Conferences may be formal or informal, short or long, public or private, teacher or student led, whole group, or one-on-one. A conference should always begin with sharing something positive about a student's drawing or writing.

Conference structure may include conversations about students' writing, teacher demonstration and guided practice, and emphasis on just one or two main areas per conference. Routman (2005) suggests the following for teacher/student writing conferences that occur before, during, or after writing:

- **Listen** to what the writer is trying to say.
- **Affirm** what the writer has done well.
- **Reinforce** the writer's strengths and attempts.
- **Assess** confusions, strengths, and next steps.
- **Teach** what's most important for the writer to move forward and only what the writer is ready for.
- **Scaffold** to help the writer say, write, and do what they can't yet do without help.
- **Set goals** with the writer's input that the writer can attempt to meet on their own, with minimal guidance and support.

Types of Conferences

Often when teachers think about teacher-student conferences, they picture students taking turns to come up to the teacher's desk to discuss their work. However, one-on-one conferencing between the teacher and students at a specific time during the writing instruction block is not the only way for students to receive feedback about their writing. Figure 3-16 identifies other types of conferences.

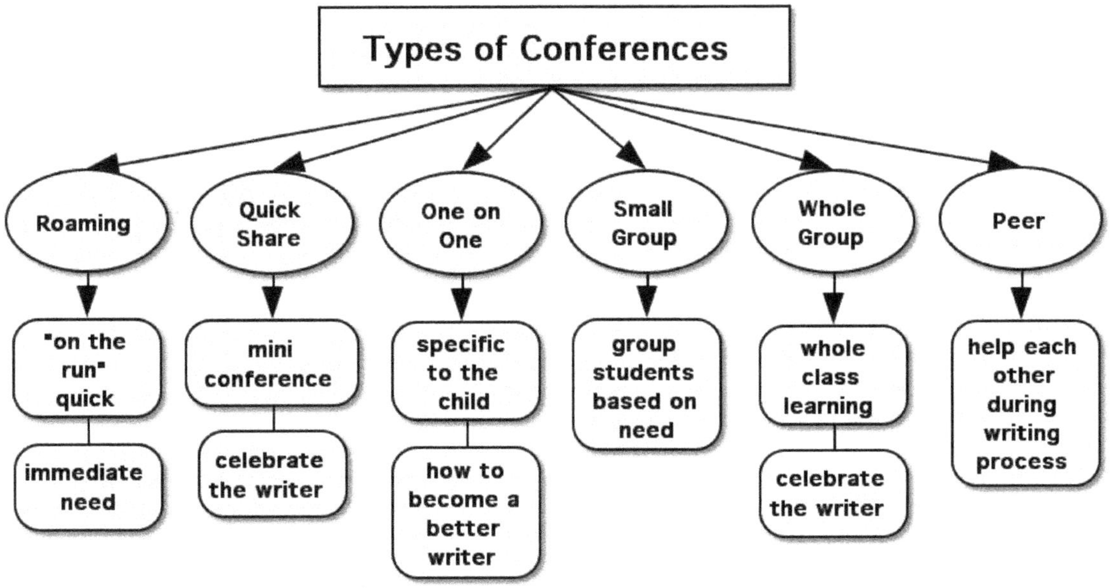

Figure 3.16

Peer Conferencing and the Language of Helpful Response

In a peer conference, students take on the role of listening to another student's writing and giving feedback. Even children in kindergarten can begin to collaborate through simple conferencing by explaining their drawings to a partner. Review the suggestions related to peer conferencing in Figure 3-17.

Figure 3-17

Peer Conferencing Suggestions

Before students conduct independent peer conferences they should:

- Observe many conferences conducted by their teacher during whole class demonstration.
- Learn how to ask thoughtful questions that help the writer.
- Be invited to give feedback with teacher guidance during whole-class sharing time.
- Observe one or more peer conferences with the whole class looking on and the teacher giving feedback.
- Try out peer conferences with the teacher nearby to give feedback.

from *Writing Essentials* by Regie Routman, 2005

Routman (2005) suggests that students can give useful and specific feedback noting what the writer has done well, what language is memorable, and what parts are interesting, confusing, or boring. However, feedback about organization, style, craft, and structure should fall primarily to teachers. Understandably, students do not have the sophisticated knowledge to give the kind of feedback that teachers can.

Students benefit from learning appropriate language for giving verbal or written feedback to their peers. Teachers can model *the language of helpful response*. That is, how to give constructive comments and positive statements about a peer's writing. Figure 3-18 lists sample sentence starters that teachers can model before asking students to use with their peers.

Figure 3-18

The Language of Helpful Response: Sentence Starters

1. Start with something positive about what the writing does: • I like the way your first sentence... • Your story reminded me of... • I could picture exactly how... • When you said … I felt... • I noticed that... • I really like the way you used...
2. Then move to what the writing has: • You tried out … • You skipped lines so you could add more words later. • You spaced your words, which makes it easy for the reader to read your message. • I like the way you used the word … instead of …
3. Use language that encourages and clarifies: • I like how you … • I saw you looking at the word wall to figure out a word. Good for you. • I hope you will continue to include lots of information in your drawings. • So, you're saying… • Can you say more about… • Perhaps you could try… • How about if you… • Let's try this together…

Two-Column Take Away: Connect to the Classroom

Add notes in the right column about instructional practices you learned in this chapter.

Stages in the Writing Process	
Collaboration	

Revision: Feedback & Conferencing	

Chapter 4
Writer's Craft and Text Structure

Successful writers combine writing skills, knowledge of text structure, and writing techniques to create an effect on the reader. Text structure is the arrangement of words in sentences, sentences in paragraphs, and the organization of larger portions of text. Writing techniques are called *writer's moves*, or *writer's craft* and involve decisions about tone (attitude), voice (writer's style and point of view), word choice, audience awareness, and use of literary devices to create an effect on the reader.

Students of any age learn how to incorporate knowledge of text structure and writing techniques into their writing by analyzing and emulating writing models, also known as *mentor text*. With support from the teacher, students in the primary grades can begin to analyze mentor text and practice using text structure and writer's craft in their drawings and writing.

Writer's Craft

Writer's craft typically refers to the language that writers use to express what they want to communicate. This includes decisions about which words to use or leave out. There are numerous writer's craft techniques used by adult writers and students in upper grades, including the use of:

- imagery, sensory details (words that appeal to one or more senses)
- figurative language (simile, metaphor)
- lead, hook
- repetition of words, phrases
- sentence variation and elaboration
- dialogue
- foreshadowing, flashback
- text features, page layout, use of graphics
- print features (bold, italic, fonts, punctuation)
- sound devices (pattern to the language such as alliteration, rhythm)
- personification (nonhuman given human characteristics)
- humor, sarcasm, satire
- hyperbole (exaggeration)
- allegory (an extended metaphor)
- narrative twist (surprise revelation)

Young students in kindergarten to grade 2 are not developmentally ready to incorporate many of the examples listed above, but they can be taught to be aware of the techniques that experienced writers employ and, in some instances, imitate them in their own drawing or writing. Writing techniques should be taught explicitly, one at a time, using several examples of mentor text.

Appropriate techniques that young students might imitate include:

- layout of text and visuals on the page

- use of illustrations, showing movement in drawings
- organization features, including headings and captions
- use of font type and size
- elaborated, descriptive language
- sentence variation
- beginning use of dialogue and quotes, using speech bubbles
- awareness of how word choice creates the writer's tone and voice

Writer's Craft: Voice

Voice refers to a writer's unique style, emotion, personality, and narrative point of view as reflected in their writing. It is sometimes described as *writing from the heart* with a goal of making the reader feel emotion. What a writer says and how it is said will convey their voice or a character's voice, as well as the overall tone of the writing piece (e.g., formal or informal, friendly, angry, sad, etc.). Instead of directly telling the reader the feeling that the writer wants to convey, voice is accomplished with carefully chosen words.

Young children can be taught to develop their own voice when drawing and writing at the sentence and eventually paragraph level. Students should be encouraged to explore writing styles, including showing their personality and point of view. Mentor texts can be shared that show how authors use voice.

An example of voice can be seen in the read aloud book *This is a Sea Cow* by Cassandra Federman (2019). In this book, the main character is a manatee who takes offense at how she is characterized by a young student who is writing a report about manatees, sometimes called *sea cows.* The student suggests that a manatee is like a land cow. As shown in the examples below, the author gives the manatee a voice by using dialogue to indicate that she is upset and defensive about what the student is saying.

- Student: *This is a sea cow.*
- Manatee's response: "Hello! I prefer 'Manatee' please."

- Student: *She is a lot like a land cow.*
- Manatee's response: "Umm, I don't think so."

- Student: *She can't see very far. Neither can cows.*
- Manatee's response: "Who's talking? Show yourself!"

- Student: *She weighs over 1,000 pounds – like a cow.*
- Manatee's response: "Hey! That's personal information."

Using Mentor Text

Mentor text can be published text, teacher writing, or samples of peer student writing. Text samples can be short (a sentence or paragraph) or as long as a whole book. One of the recommendations in the Institute of Education Sciences research report (Graham et al., 2012) includes teaching students to emulate the features of good writing. The report explains:

> "Students should be exposed to exemplary texts from a variety of sources, including published or professional texts, books, and textbooks, the teacher's own writing, and peer samples. Teachers should select texts that
>
> - support the instructional goals of the lesson,
> - are appropriate for students' reading levels and abilities,
> - and provide exemplary models of what students will write.
>
> Exemplary texts can illustrate a number of features, including text structure; use of graphs, charts, and pictures; effective word choice; and varied sentence structure. Teachers should either read exemplary texts out loud or direct students to read and reread selected exemplary texts, paying close attention to the author's word choice, overall structure, or other style elements. Teachers should explain and students should discuss how each text demonstrates characteristics of effective writing in that particular genre. Students will then be prepared to emulate characteristics of exemplary texts at the word, sentence and/or text level, or they can use the text as a springboard for writing." (p. 22)

As the report notes, teachers can use read aloud or have students read mentor text if they have sufficient reading skills. The focus of attention can vary, including an element of text structure (e.g., introductions, transition words), a pattern of organization (e.g., description, sequence, compare and contrast), or examples of writing craft (e.g., voice, word choice, awareness of audience).

It is important to select mentor text that is developmentally appropriate and provides clear examples of the writing structure or technique that is the focus of instruction. As noted above, it is not necessary to share a full text; a few sentences or a short passage may be sufficient for students to analyze and copy. It is helpful to show more than one mentor text sample.

Reading Like a Writer

One of the benefits of purposely using mentor text is that it strengthens students' self-image as writers because they see themselves creating the same type of writing as published authors (Glover, 2014). When teachers ask students to analyze text with the explained purpose of imitating something about how the author wrote that text, students start to *read like a writer*.

Whenever the teacher uses read aloud or students read themselves, it is helpful to take a moment to have students focus on some aspect related to the choices made by the author. When this begins in the early grades, students develop a habit of mind to notice and think about how text is written.

Mentor Text Routine

When using mentor text, follow the routine detailed in Figure 4-1 that is aligned with the *Launch, Explore, Land* writing lesson routine. Figure 4-2 is an example of an anchor chart that can be used during the lesson.

Figure 4-1

Routine for Using Mentor Text

LAUNCH	1. Select one or more texts or a part of texts that highlight a specific text structure or writing technique. 2. Have students read or listen to the sample text. 3. Point out the structure or technique and share your thinking about it. 4. Lead a discussion about how students might emulate it. 5. Model how to use it using think aloud.
EXPLORE	6. Provide an opportunity for students to employ it in their own writing, independently or in collaboration with other students. 7. Provide a scaffold if needed (e.g., template, word list, graphic organizer).
LAND	8. Come back together to share and reflect on learning.

Figure 4-2

Learning about: ______________________			
Mentor Text: Title, Author	What do we notice?	Why was it used?	Try it!

Where can you find mentor text?

Mentor text can be samples of published text written by expert authors that are found in books, articles, magazines, websites, and classroom reading material. Mentor text can also be samples written by teachers or students. Keep in mind that the same mentor text can be used to highlight different skills and strategies. Here are some suggestions:

- Your classroom: The first place to look is in your classroom. What reading materials are you already using that can be used to provide examples of text structure or techniques?
- Start a Collection: Be on the lookout for samples of text that you think will be useful and start a collection for future use. Organize sample text by elements.
- Use Mentor Text Resources: There are a number of books and websites you can consult that offer mentor text suggestions.

Text Structure: The Three Types of Writing

Teaching students about text structure supports both writing and reading comprehension. When students are aware of the structure of a text they are reading, they recognize how the author built the text. This knowledge provides clues to meaning. Conversely, students need an awareness of text structure to build a piece of their own writing in a way that helps readers understand what they are trying to convey.

Genre-Specific Writing

Genre is a kind or type of writing that serves a specific purpose. The Common Core State Standards identify three major types (genres) of writing that students in all grades must learn to write: *opinion* (grades kindergarten through 5) or *argument* (grades 6-12), *informational*, and *narrative*. Figure 4-3 lists the grade-specific standards for the three types of writing, which make up the first three of the ten writing standards.

Figure 4-3

Common Core Writing Standards

Writing Standard #1: Opinion Writing

Anchor Standard: *Write arguments to support claims in an analysis of substantive topics or texts, using valid reasoning and relevant and sufficient evidence.*

Kindergarten: Use a combination of drawing, dictating, and writing to compose opinion pieces in which they tell a reader the topic or the name of the book they are writing about and state an opinion or preference about the topic or book (e.g., *My favorite book is . . .*).

Grade 1: Write opinion pieces in which they introduce the topic or name the book they are writing about, state an opinion, supply a reason for the opinion, and provide some sense of closure.

Grade 2: Write opinion pieces in which they introduce the topic or book they are writing about, state an opinion, supply reasons that support the opinion, use linking words (e.g., *because, and, also*) to connect opinion and reasons, and provide a concluding statement or section.

Writing Standard #2: Informational Writing

<u>*Anchor Standard:*</u> *Write informative/explanatory texts to examine and convey complex ideas and information clearly and accurately through the effective selection, organization, and analysis of content.*

Kindergarten: Use a combination of drawing, dictating, and writing to compose informative/explanatory texts in which they name what they are writing about and supply some information about the topic.

Grade 1: Write informative/explanatory texts in which they name a topic, supply some facts about the topic, and provide some sense of closure.

Grade 2: Write informative/explanatory texts in which they introduce a topic, use facts and definitions to develop points, and provide a concluding statement or section.

Writing Standard #3: Narrative Writing

<u>*Anchor Standard:*</u> *Write narratives to develop real or imagined experiences or events using effective technique, well-chosen details, and well-structured event sequences.*

Kindergarten: Use a combination of drawing, dictating, and writing to narrate a single event or several loosely linked events, tell about the events in the order in which they occurred, and provide a reaction to what happened.

Grade 1: Write narratives in which they recount two or more appropriately sequenced events, include some details regarding what happened, use temporal words to signal event order, and provide some sense of closure.

Grade 2: Write narratives in which they recount a well-elaborated event or short sequence of events, include details to describe actions, thoughts, and feelings, use temporal words to signal event order, and provide a sense of closure.

<u>*Sub-Genres*</u>

There are additional, more specific genres that are found within the three main types of writing, such as poetry, fable, biography, memoir, etc. There is also a wide variety of writing tasks that can be assigned to young students within the three types of writing. For example:

- <u>Opinion:</u> persuasive letter, book or movie review, opinion of characters in a story, "my favorite ___ is ___"

- Informational: labels on drawings or illustrations, lists of facts or information, letters, invitations and cards, description, directions, response to a question
- Narrative: personal narrative, story or retell of a story, daily journal, contribution to a class story

Three Types of Writing: Purpose

It is important for students to recognize the overall purpose of each type of writing. When students understand the connection between genres and writing purposes, they will be more likely to use different genres and think more critically about how to structure their writing (Graham et al., 2012). Figure 4-4 shows an example of a graphic that can be shared with students to help them

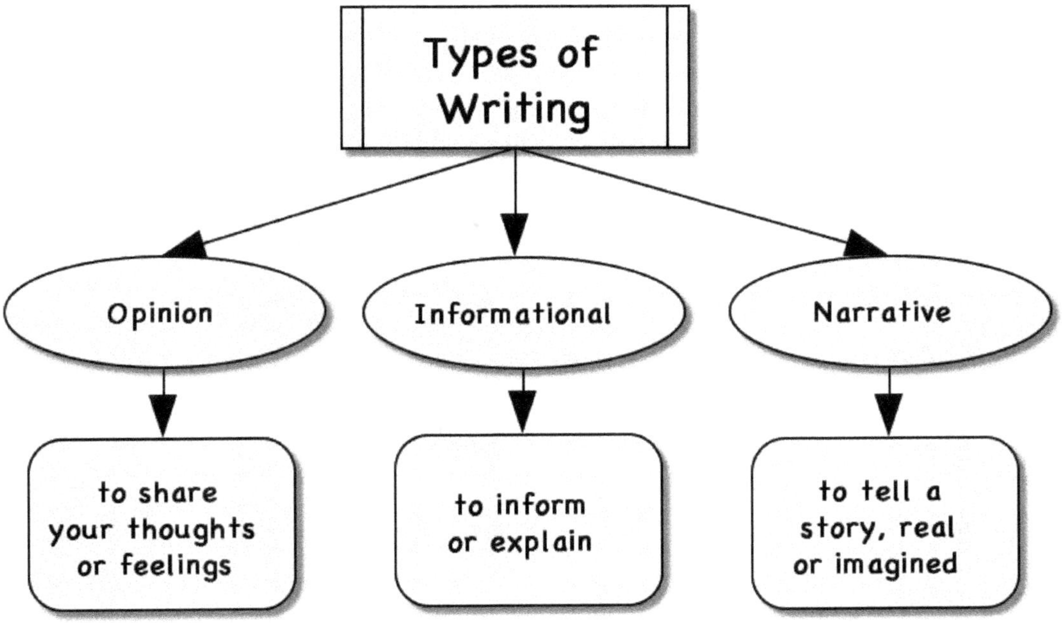

remember the purpose for opinion, informational, and narrative writing.

Figure 4-4

The Common Core state standards suggest that students in elementary grades spend *equal time* on each of the writing types (CCSS, 2010, p.5) and emphasize that this can be achieved by incorporating more informational and opinion writing during science, social studies, and other subjects to balance out the common emphasis on narrative writing during the language arts/literacy block. However, there is a shift as students move into middle and high school. By high school, the standards suggest that student writing be 40% argument, 40% informational, and 20% narrative.

Text Structure: Opinion Writing

Opinion writing in primary grades presents, shares, or conveys a point of view or opinion. It is helpful to explain to students that this type of writing provides a way for the writer to share their own preferences and feelings. Teachers can show examples of opinion writing using mentor text (see the suggestions in the Appendix). Young students begin in kindergarten by using a drawing and a few words to state an opinion or preference about a topic or a book.

Opinion writing relies on a student's ability to think critically about information that might be used to support an opinion. It is helpful to have students use oral rehearsal prior to drawing or writing because it provides an opportunity to hear others' perspectives, clarify thinking, and practice using academic vocabulary. Figure 4-5 reviews the characteristics of opinion text.

Figure 4-5

Opinion Text

Purpose	present, share, or convey a point of view or opinion; share your thoughts or feelings
Structure	opinion structure is organized around these components: topic, statement of opinion or point of view, reasons that support the opinion
Examples	opinion letters, book or movie reviews, stories in which characters express their opinion

The Difference Between Persuasion & Opinion

Some writing programs use the term *persuasive writing* instead of *opinion writing*. There is a subtle difference between these terms.

- The focus for **opinion** writing in the Common Core writing standards:
  - Present, share, or convey a point of view or opinion; share your thoughts or feelings
  - Based on solid reasons
  - Example: Why I love my dog:
    - *She calms me.*
    - *She is warm and cute.*
    - *She keeps me safe.*
- The focus for **persuasive** writing:
  - State an opinion and convince the reader to support it
  - Based on solid reasons, might appeal to the reader's emotions and feelings
  - Example: Why you should love dogs:
    - *They teach you responsibility.*
    - *Dog walking keeps you fit.*

- *Dogs can protect your home.*

Text Structure: Informational Writing

For primary students, informational writing affords an opportunity to write about what they know and what they are learning in school. It also provides an opportunity to incorporate academic vocabulary that students are learning related to science, social studies, and other subjects. Teachers can show examples of informational writing using mentor text (see suggestions in the Appendix). Kindergarten students begin by labeling their drawings or giving facts and information in short sentences. Figure 4-6 reviews the characteristics of informational writing.

Figure 4-6

Informational Text

Purpose	examines previously learned information or provides new information
Structure	information tends to be organized into topics or main ideas that are presented hierarchically
Examples	letters, biographies, how-to-books, directions, alphabet books, retell and summary writing, print and digital articles, nonfiction books on math, science, and social studies topics

Text Structure: Narrative Writing

Narrative writing tells a story that is real or imagined. When explaining narrative writing, teachers should remind students that narrative writing is a way for a writer to share a story, most often based on an event or a series of events. Generally, narrative writing is sequential in primary grades (i.e., no flashbacks) and there is a clear beginning, middle and end to a writing piece. Many primary students tend to produce personal narratives, but teachers should assign other types of narrative writing. Teachers can show examples of narrative writing using mentor text (see suggestions in the Appendix). Figure 4-7 reviews the characteristics of narrative writing.

Figure 4-7

Narrative Text

Purpose	tells a story (real or imagined) or an experience, event, or sequence of events
Structure	narrative structure is organized around a beginning, middle, and end
Examples	diary or journal entry, biography or autobiography, personal narrative, folktales, fables, myths, creative fictional stories, plays

Narrative writing in kindergarten begins with a drawing and words related to a single event. The Common Core writing standards require a progression of narrative writing that increases in complexity as students write about multiple events and incorporate more story elements in their writing. By third grade, students are expected to establish a situation, introduce characters, organize an event sequence, use dialogue and descriptions, and use temporal transition words as they develop their own narratives.

Early Development of Text Genres

Coker and Ritchey (2015, p. 15-20) note the following about the research on writing development in kindergarten through grade two:

- Children learn to produce specific genres gradually. Early forms of stories or informational text may not look like mature forms, but they contain some of the genre's characteristics. For example, a story may be represented by a list of events, and informational writing may start with one or two details about a single topic.
- Skill with each genre develops separately. A student who writes excellent stories may not be as strong writing informational or opinion text. It is therefore important to provide specific instruction for each type of writing.
- Students' writing achievement appears to be related to their experience with the genre. They become better writers of a genre when they have many opportunities to read texts (or hear read aloud) of that genre. Teachers should select text for reading with this in mind.
- Students' writing achievement is related to their ability to produce genres orally. If they can tell better stories orally, their written narratives will be longer, contain more narrative elements (characters, setting, events) and be more interesting. If they can present information orally, their informational writing pieces will contain more detail.
- Opinion Writing: In kindergarten and grade one writers express a clear opinion and include evidence for their opinion. First grade students have demonstrated that they can write an opinion essay with a claim. Students often produce better oral opinions than written ones, likely because of the challenges of spelling and handwriting.
- Informational Writing: Studies show a progression in the structure of informational writing that begins with simple labels that name or briefly describe an object or topic. Next, students include descriptions of the topic that become more elaborated and organized. Later, more complex text is organized into paragraphs that include important transitions among ideas and between paragraphs. The progression often develops as follows:
  - word or sentence used to identify aspects of a picture
  - clause or sentence going beyond labeling the picture, maybe introducing a topic
  - two or more clauses related to a single topic
  - two or more attribute lists created for subtopics of a larger topic
  - a collection of two, related statements serving as subtopics which begin to include more supporting evidence and explanation
  - paragraphs that introduce a topic and subtopic with several connected sentences

- Narrative Writing: Narrative skills do not develop at the same rate for all students; research shows that even some upper elementary students still write simple narratives.

Text Features

Authors use *text features* to organize information and ideas and highlight important parts of a text. Text features include elements such as a title, headings, illustrations or graphics, maps or charts, captions, and bold or italic print. A *table of contents* is also considered a text feature.
The title helps identify the topic. Headings represent topical sections of a text, making it easier for readers to work their way through a longer piece of text in manageable "chunks". Headings also help writers organize their ideas into related sub-topics. Illustrations, graphics, maps, and charts present an alternative visual representation of the text. Bold and italic print are used to highlight key terms and concepts. The table of contents offers a clue to the organization of a text.

Young students as early as kindergarten are able to incorporate text features into their writing, as shown in the student writing sample in Figure 4-8. Teachers should share mentor text examples that include examples of text features for students to emulate.

Figure 4-8

Use of Text Features: Kindergarten Student Example

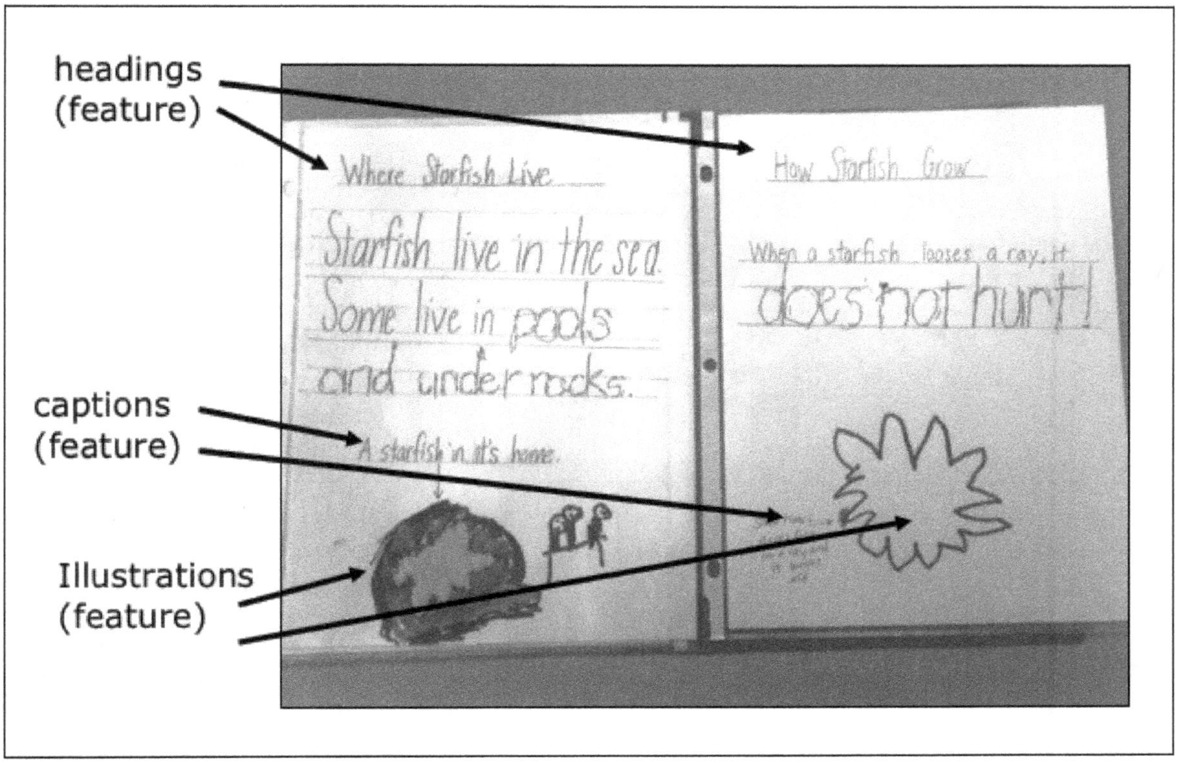

Introduction, Body Development, Conclusion

The first three Common Core writing standards include details about introductions, body development, and conclusions. Keep the following questions in mind as you review the grade-specific details for kindergarten through grade 2 in Figure 4-9:

- What do you notice about the requirements for introduction, body and conclusion as students move from kindergarten into grade 2?
- Compare and contrast what is expected for introduction, body development, and conclusion in narrative, informational, and opinion writing.

Figure 4-9

Introduction			
grade	*Opinion* *Standard 1*	*Informational* *Standard 2*	*Narrative* *Standard 3*
K	Tell topic or name book, state opinion or preference	Name what they are writing about	Starts in grade 3
1	Introduce topic or name book, state opinion	Name the topic	Starts in grade 3
2	Introduce topic or book, state opinion	Name the topic	Starts in grade 3
Body Development			
grade	*Opinion*	*Informational*	*Narrative*
K	Use drawing, dictating, and writing to compose an opinion piece	Use drawing, dictating, and writing to compose informative texts, supply some information about the topic	Use drawing, dictating, and writing to narrate a single event or several loosely linked events, tell about the events in the order in which they occurred, provide a reaction to what happened
1	Supply a reason for the opinion	Supply some facts about the topic	Recount two or more appropriately sequenced events, include some details about what happened, use temporal words to signal event order

2	Supply reasons that support the opinion, use linking words to connect opinion and reasons	Use facts and definitions to develop points	Recount a well elaborated event or short sequence of events, include details to describe actions, thoughts, and feelings, use temporal words to signal event order
		Conclusion	
grade	*Opinion*	*Informational*	*Narrative*
K	Starts in grade 1		
1	Provide some sense of closure		
2	Provide a concluding statement or section		Provide a sense of closure

Introductions and Conclusions

The basic purpose of an introduction is to let the reader know what the writing is about. The basic purpose of a conclusion, sometimes called an ending, is to provide the reader with a sense of closure. Kindergarten and grade 1 students may use just a few words for an introduction or a conclusion, but as students move into upper grades their introductions and conclusions might range from one sentence to more than a paragraph, depending on the writing task.

Body Development

As shown in the details for the Common Core writing standards in Figure 4-9, the body development and structure for the three types of writing varies. Opinion text is organized around reasons, informational text around information and facts, and narrative text around events.

Topic Web Graphic Organizer

A *topic web* is a graphic organizer that can be used to teach students about text structure for the three types of writing, emphasizing the components of introduction, body development, and conclusion. It can also be used as a tool for planning before writing (see Chapters 7 and 8). Figure 4-10 illustrates two versions of a topic web. The first is used for informational or opinion text, and the second for narrative text. These topic webs can be used to represent the text structure of a mentor text, or to plan a writing piece.

Figure 4-10

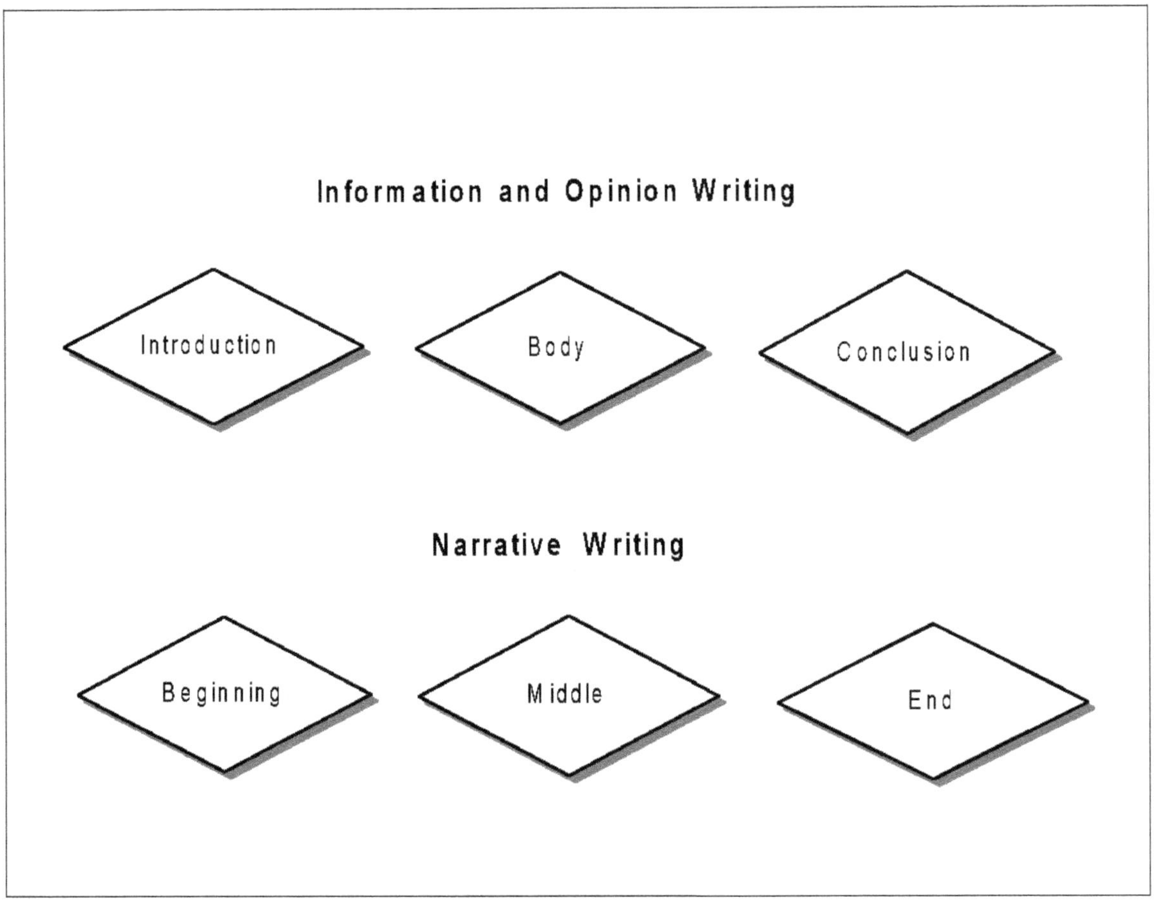

Topic Webs to Show Informational Structure

Informational text tends to be organized into topics or main ideas that are presented hierarchically. An informational topic web will start at the top with the basic *introduction*, *body*, and *conclusion* components. The body is developed by adding shapes representing main ideas and details. The number of main ideas can vary. The first sample topic web in Figure 4-11 represents a single, informational paragraph, of the type a first or second grade student might write. The first sentence is the introduction – the topic of the paragraph is stated there. There are three body sentences, with one detail represented in each. The final sentence is the concluding sentence which provides some closure to the paragraph.

The second topic web in Figure 4-11 represents a multi-paragraph text, something a second or third grade student might write. The introduction can be one or more sentences. The body has three paragraphs represented by the three main ideas. Each paragraph includes supporting sentences with details related to the main idea. The conclusion can be one or more sentences that provide closure to the writing piece.

Figure 4-11

Informational Topic Webs

Single Paragraph

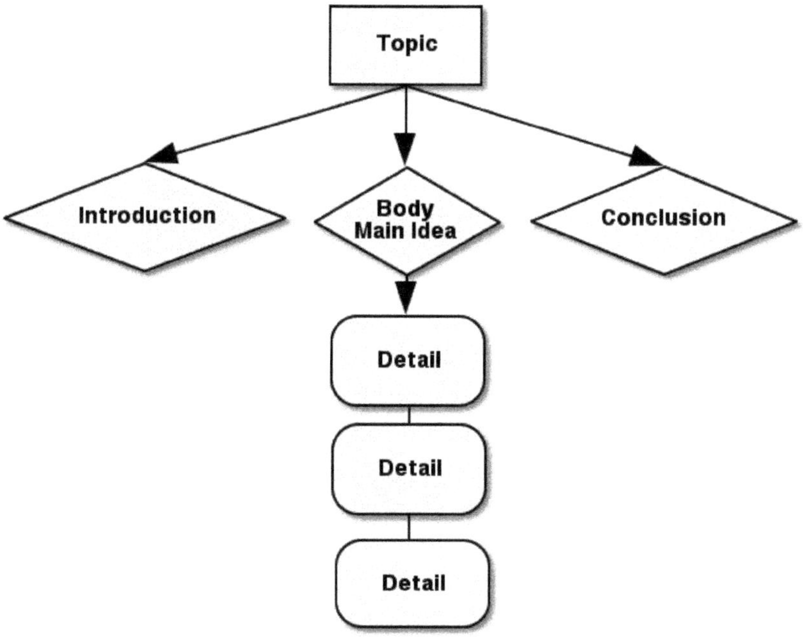

Multiple Paragraphs

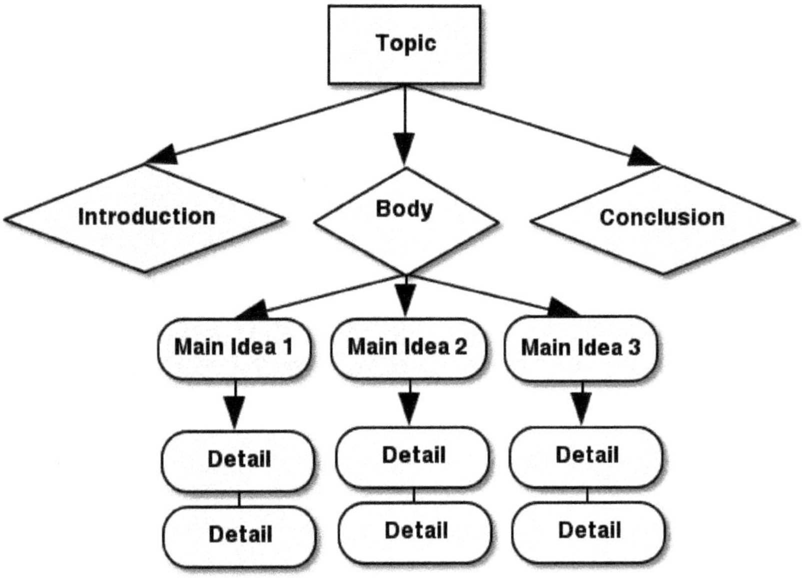

Reading Like a Writer: Topic Webs for Sample Informational Text

Teachers can use a topic web to represent the structure of mentor informational text. The questions below can be used to help students *read like a writer*. Figure 4-12 shows an example of a topic web that represents the structure of a mentor informational text.

- Introduction
  - Did the author identify the topic of the piece?
- Body
  - How many main ideas are in the body?
  - Are there any text features?
- Conclusion
  - Did the author provide a sense of closure?

Figure 4-12

How to Fix Up a Yard

Try these five ways to make a yard nice.

One way is by planting plenty of trees. Trees make spots of shade, so you can rest if the sun is hot. Pine trees have a nice fresh smell.

Make flower beds in lots of places. I planted pink and red roses on all sides of my yard. Roses smell so sweet!

Be wise and cut the grass as it starts to get tall, or it will soon look messy. Cutting it again in a week or so will keep it short.

Get rid of weeds! Weeds will grow fast in summer and make a yard look bad. It can be hard to dig them up, but you will be glad you did.

Did you do all these jobs? Then it is time for the last task. Set a bench under a tree so you can sit and chat with pals. That is the best part of keeping a fine yard!

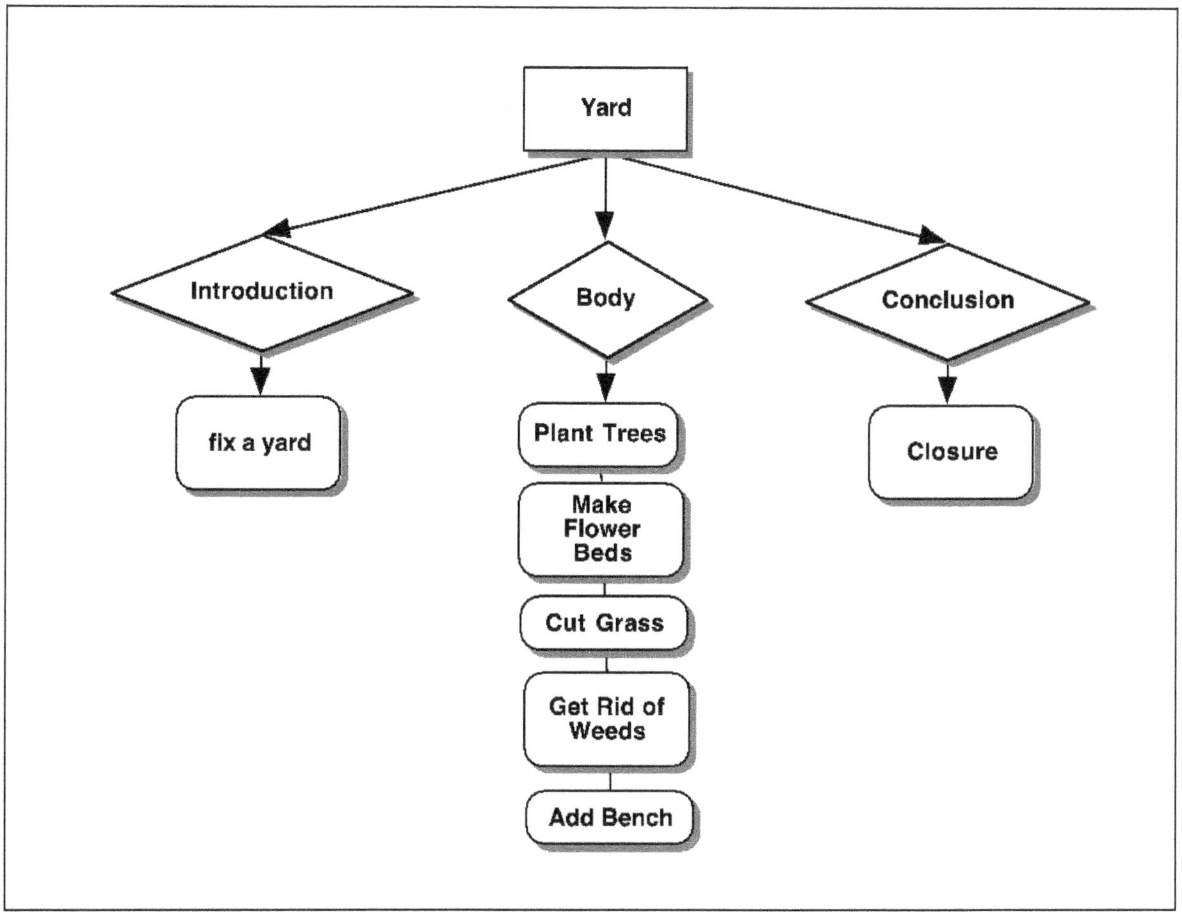

Topic Webs to Show Opinion Structure

Opinion text tends to be organized around the statement of an opinion and the reasons that support the opinion. An opinion topic web will start at the top with the basic *introduction*, *body*, and *conclusion* components. The body is developed by adding shapes representing reasons to support the opinion. The number of reasons can vary. Figure 4-13 can be used to represent single or multi-paragraph opinion text. The first sentence is the introduction – the topic and the opinion are stated there. The body of the text includes three reasons that support the opinion. The number of reasons may vary. The concluding sentence provides some closure.

Figure 4-13

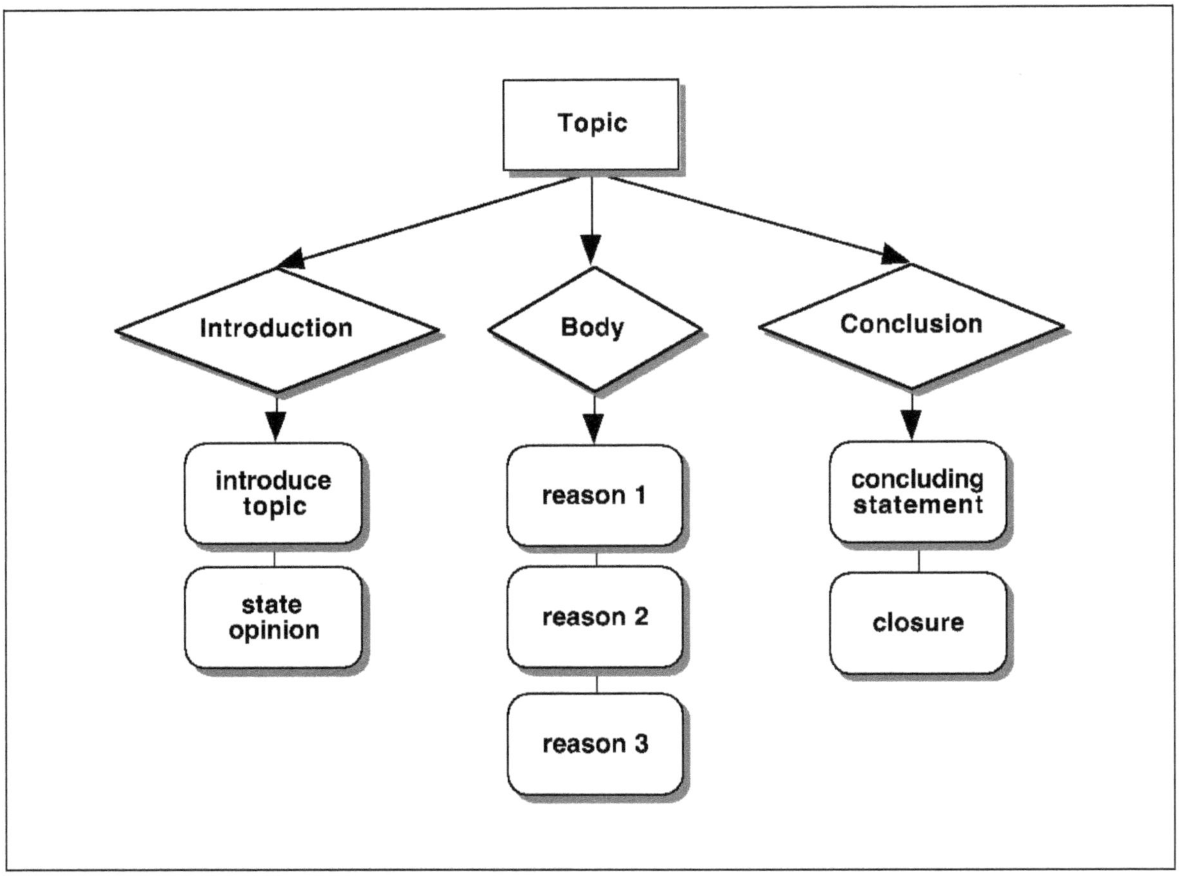

Reading Like a Writer: Topic Webs for Sample Opinion Text

Teachers can use a topic web to represent the structure of mentor opinion text. The questions below can be used to help students *read like a writer*. Figure 4-14 shows an example of a topic web that represents the structure of a mentor informational text.

- Introduction
  - Did the author clearly identify the topic of the piece?
  - Did the author state the opinion or point of view?
- Body
  - Did the author provide reasons to support the opinion?
- Conclusion
  - Did the author provide a sense of closure?

Figure 4-14

Restaurant Review – Crumbs Bakery

"This is the best vanilla cupcake I ever had," said a little boy sitting at the table next to me at Crumbs Bakery on the Upper West Side. I agreed. Crumbs is the best bakery for cupcakes!

Crumbs is the best bakery in my neighborhood because they have a beautiful display of all their cupcakes so you can see what is available.

The people who work at Crumbs are always friendly.

Another reason Crumbs is the best bakery is that the cupcakes are sweet but not too sweet, with the perfect amount of frosting, about a half of an inch!

Crumbs is the best bakery for cupcakes. It gets five stars out of five!

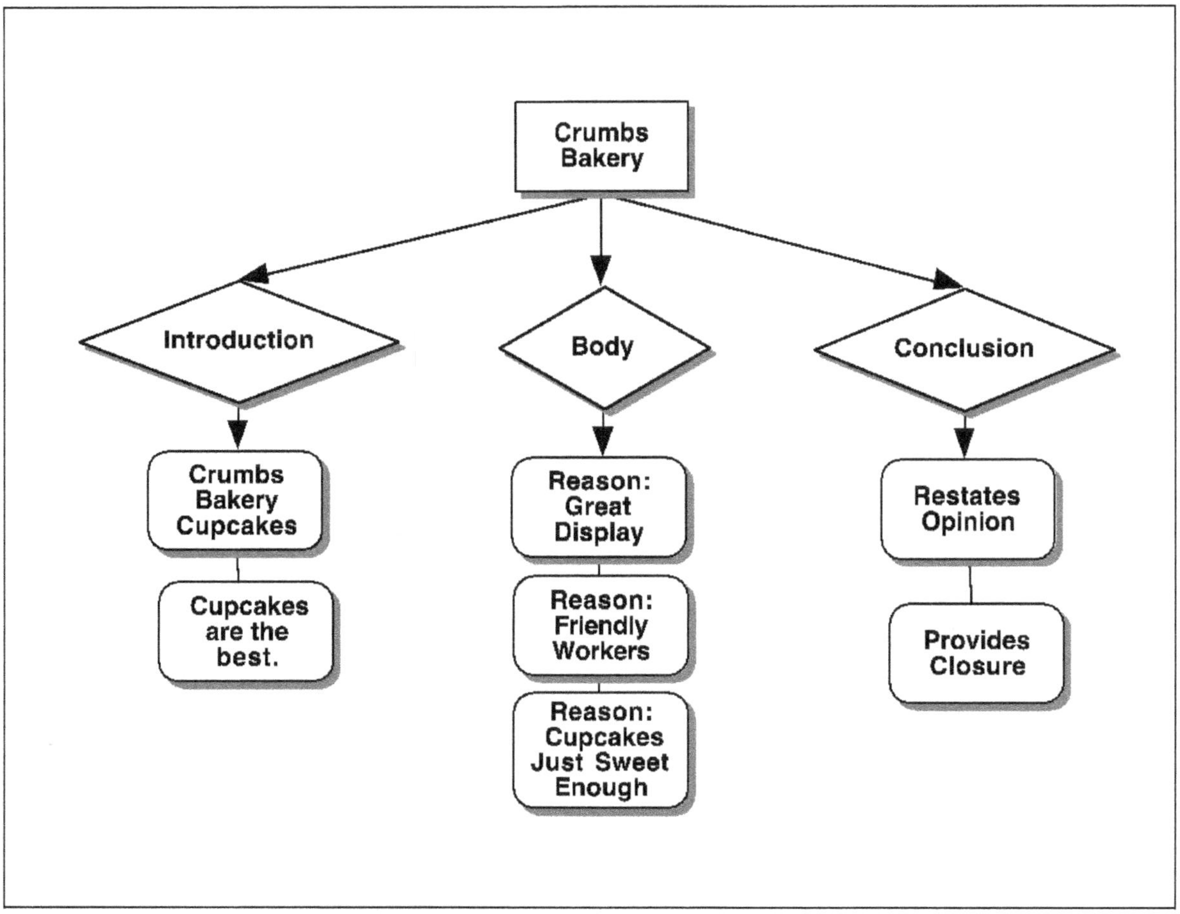

Topic Webs to Show Narrative Structure

Narrative text tends to be structured around a series of events occurring in order that can be organized into a topic web representing *beginning, middle*, and *end*. The *middle* (body) of the narrative is developed by adding shapes representing events. The topic web in Figure 4-15 represents narrative text that has four main events. The number of events can vary. At the *beginning* of narrative text, the writer establishes a situation or introduces a narrator or character. At the *end*, the writer brings some closure to the narrative.

Figure 4-15

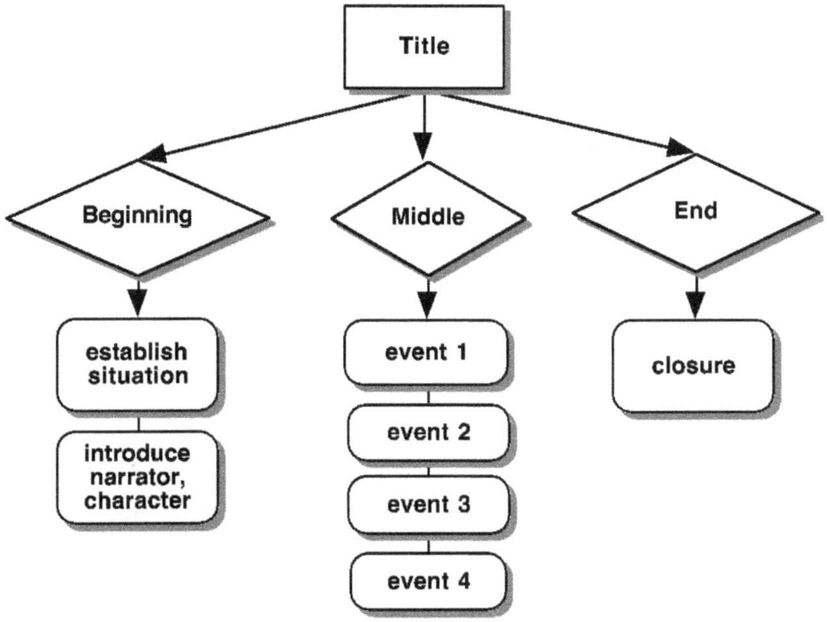

Reading Like a Writer: Topic Webs for Sample Narrative Text

Teachers can use a topic web to represent the structure of mentor narrative text. The questions below can be used to help students *read like a writer*. Figure 4-16 shows an example of a topic web that represents the structure of a mentor narrative text.

- Beginning
  - Did the author establish a situation?
  - Did the author introduce characters or a narrator?
- Middle
  - Did the author present the events in a logical order?
  - Did the author include dialogue?
- End
  - Did the author provide a sense of closure?

Figure 4-16

The Lion and the Mouse
Retold by Claire Daniel

One day Mouse bumped into Lion by mistake and woke him up. Lion caught Mouse and dangled him by his tail.

"Do not eat me!" Mouse cried. "One day I will return the favor."

Lion laughed so hard that he dropped Mouse. Lion said, "How can a tiny mouse ever help a mighty lion like me?"

The next day Lion fell into a hunter's trap. He was covered with a net. Lion's roars shook the ground.

Other animals heard Lion, but no one wanted to come near an angry lion. Only Mouse ran toward Lion.

Mouse said, "I will help you."

Lion roared, "You are too small to help me!"

Mouse just said, "Lion be quiet."

Mouse chewed the net. He chewed for a long time. Finally, Mouse made a hole. Lion was free!

Just then the hunters returned. Lion roared at the men, and they ran away. One hunter looked back. He saw the proud lion walking away. Then he rubbed his eyes. Could it be? A mouse was riding on the lion's back!

Lion and Mouse became best friends. Lion liked to say, "Little friends can make the best friends."

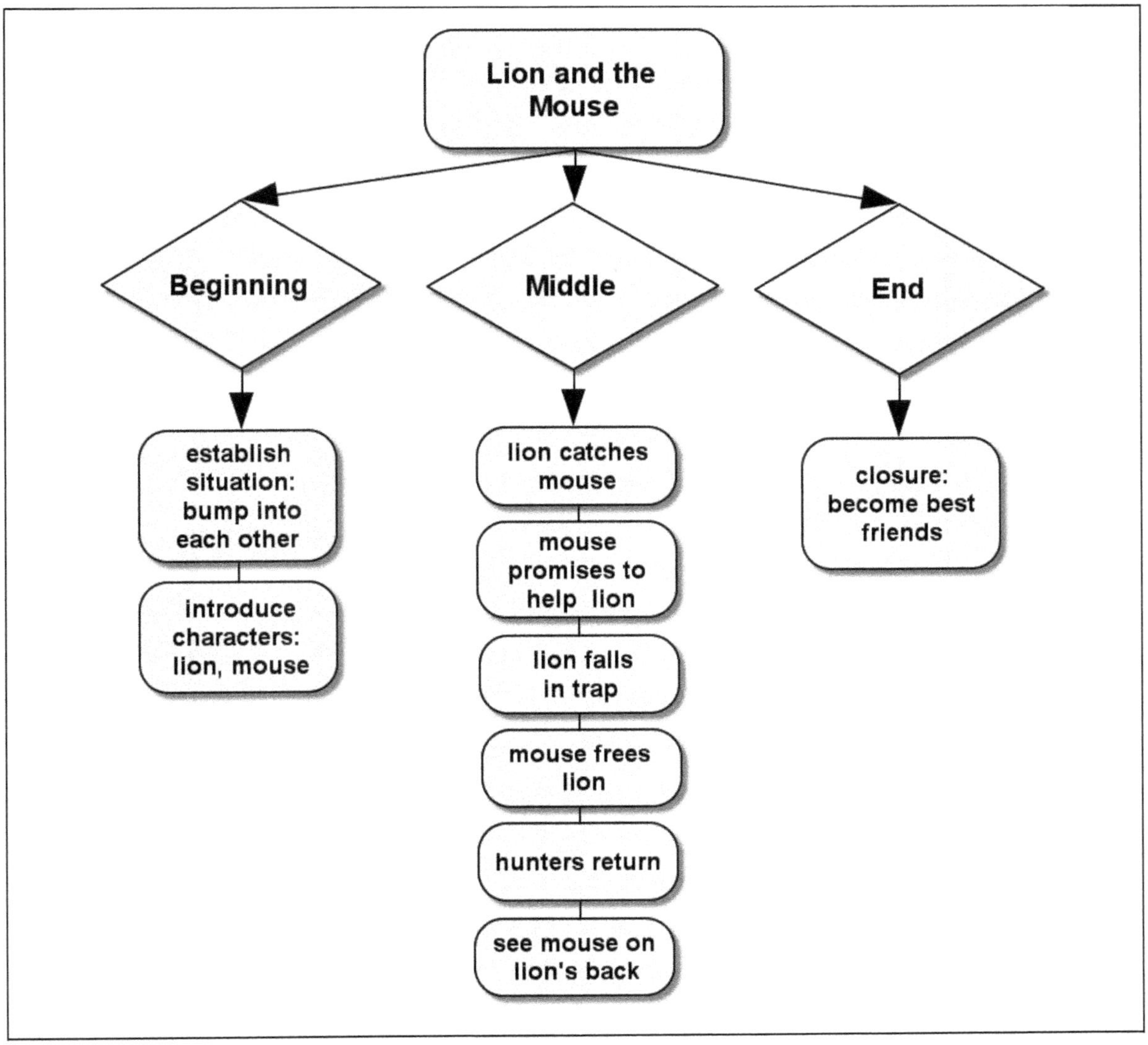

Two-Column Take Away: Connect to the Classroom

Add notes in the right column about instructional practices you learned in this chapter.

Mentor Text 3 Types of Writing	

Text Structure: Text Features, Introduction, Body, Conclusion Topic Webs to Represent Text Structure	

Chapter 5
Drawing, Labels, Lists

Drawing is a critical stage in beginning writing – it is an important milestone as young children learn to write. The Common Core kindergarten writing standards for opinion, informational, and narrative writing note that students should *use drawing, dictating, and writing to compose*, and drawing continues to be an important part of the composing process into grade 1.

Graham and colleagues (2012) point out that from a developmental standpoint, drawing is a foundational writing skill that leads to the application of more sophisticated techniques. They note:

> "For younger students, writing activities could include interpretive drawings, invented spelling, or interactive writing. Although these activities are not often considered traditional writing experiences, they accomplish the same goals: helping students communicate thoughts and ideas to others, encouraging them to engage with the text to deepen their understanding of the content, and drawing connections to prior learning experiences." (p. 6)

The act of drawing and talking about a drawing provide a supportive scaffold within which students can construct a piece of writing. By using a single word with a picture, a student is able to convey a story because most of the meaning is carried by the picture.

A typical progression for beginning composing follows these stages:

- Scribbling random marks on a page
- Drawing illustrations
- Dictating ideas and thoughts to a teacher who scribes
- Labeling objects and illustrations
- Combining words and pictures
- Adding phrases and sentences

First drawings may consist of a few objects placed on the page. Later, students attempt to show action by adding arrows or lines to show characters moving or interacting with one another.

Oral Rehearsal for Writing: From Talk to Text

Talking supports writing in several ways. Students use discussion with others to generate ideas about what they want to say in their writing. When they are finished writing, they can use talk to reflect on their writing, which can lead to revision.

Another important way that young students use talk is to orally rehearse (vocalize) what they want to say prior to writing. This is sometimes referred to as *say it, write it.* Students use talk to support moving from their thoughts to spoken words, and then the spoken words to writing. Myhil and Jones (2009) note the following about oral rehearsal prior to writing:

- Students practice producing written text in oral form by saying aloud what they intend to write in precisely the way it will be written.
- Oral rehearsal offers students a chance to shape and reframe phrases or sentences they will write.
- Students can use oral rehearsal both as an individual rehearsal process and as an interactive shared process with peers.
- By drawing on their spoken language production, oral rehearsal may reduce the cognitive load of spelling and handwriting while writing because the phrase or sentence has already been shaped.
- Oral rehearsal is the *idea bridge* between creative, content-forming talk used to generate ideas and the more scripted nature of writing.

Talk to text is especially helpful for students in kindergarten and the beginning of grade 1 when their spelling and handwriting skills are not sufficiently developed to enable them to capture in written words what they want to say.

Drawing and the Writing Process

Even if young students are using just a few words, or perhaps no words at all, they should still be encouraged to follow the stages of the writing process when they compose using drawing as described below.

- Think/Plan:
  - *What will the drawing be about?*
  - *What details should be included?*
- Write:
  - *Complete the drawing*
  - *Add words*
- Revise:
  - *Elaborate the drawing – add more detail*
  - *Add more words*

Drawing Instruction

Teachers should not assume that their students know how to draw or draw well enough to convey the ideas they want to express. Sometimes students are reluctant to draw because they are not confident in their drawing skills. They may become frustrated because they cannot make a drawing look like professional drawings they see in books, or they may be worried that others will "make fun" of their drawings. As noted in Chapter 2, an important part of developing a community of writers is providing an environment where students support each other's attempts at drawing and writing.

The *Launch* stage of the writing lesson is a good time to provide explicit instruction for drawing skills, including how to draw basic shapes (e.g., circle, triangle, square) that form the foundation of student drawings. Teachers can also teach students how to elaborate and add more to their drawings to help others understand the message in a drawing. For example, the teacher might focus on drawing people, including:

- how to use simple shapes for the head, body, legs, and arms
- including colors and patterns for clothes
- adding details such as hair, hands, fingernails, shoes, eyelashes

The examples in Figure 5-1 depict practice for drawing a cat and an owl using basic shapes. Read aloud books devoted to motivating young students to compose through their drawing can be helpful (see a suggested list in the Appendix).

Figure 5-1

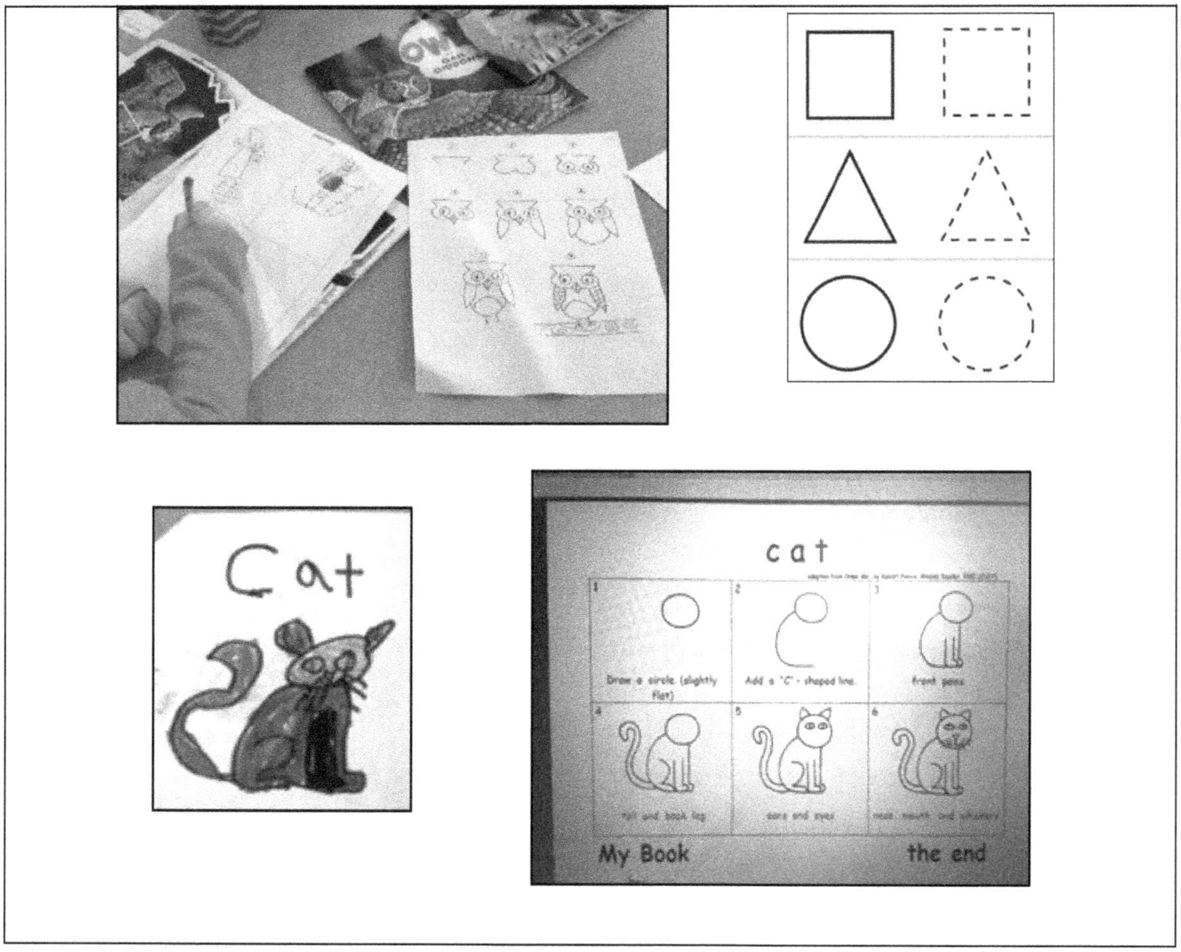

Adding Words Through Dictation

Before students are able to write phrases and sentences, teachers can ask them to dictate what they want to say about their drawing and the teacher writes the words. The teacher and student might also *share the pen* and do an interactive writing of the words. Figure 5-2 includes samples of student drawings that include wording that was added by the teacher.

Figure 5-2

Picture Book Making

For this activity, students create a series of drawings (with or without written words) that are combined into an informational or narrative book. As they make these books, young students have an opportunity to try on the roles of writers and illustrators. Figure 5-3 shows an informational book about ladybugs.

Figure 5-3

Illustration Study Using Mentor Books

An illustration study is an activity that asks students to study the visuals in mentor books, typically those that are used for read-aloud in kindergarten and grade 1 (see examples in the Appendix). The goal is to develop an awareness of the role that illustration can play in conveying what a writer wants to say. Begin an illustration study lesson by showing one or two mentor examples of a particular technique (writer's craft), and then ask students what they notice and find interesting about the examples. Students can share their reactions in whole or small group discussions. Then provide an opportunity for students to imitate the technique in their own drawings. Examples of illustration and visual techniques used by authors include:

- using only pictures to tell a story
- labeling parts of illustrations
- adding lines and other markings to indicate that people or objects are moving
- purposely using color in illustrations to express meaning
- changing the shape, size, and style of letters in words
- using perspective – zooming in and out
- including background details – location, time of day, weather, or season
- using multiple illustrations on one page or spreading an illustration across pages

Labels and Lists

The first words that young students add to their drawings will be one- or two-word labels. The next developmental step before writing phrases and sentences is making lists of words or names. The teacher can model by labeling items in the classroom and making lists together with students. Mentor texts that have examples of authors using labels and lists are also helpful (see a suggested list in the Appendix).

Students benefit from practice with labeling and making lists. Labeling and listing activities can be included in learning centers where students have an opportunity to practice with peers. For example:

- drawings to label at the science center
- items to label at the dramatic play center
- a list of items to purchase at the classroom store
- a list of people to send cards or letters at the classroom post office
- supplies to label or list in the art center

Invented Spelling, Spelling Supports

Chapter 1 addressed the role that *transcription skills* (spelling and handwriting) play in learning how to write. Suggestions for teaching spelling and handwriting were summarized in that chapter, along with an explanation of *invented spelling* (young students' best attempts to spell words). Keep in mind that students will employ invented spelling when they begin writing labels and lists. Many students avoid writing a word (or they replace a more sophisticated word with a simple word) because they do not know how to spell it. In addition to encouraging students to use invented spelling, teachers can provide the following resources to support spelling in primary grade classrooms:

- **Word lists:** Post lists of high-frequency words, words related to topics that students are writing about, and words with recently learned phonics concepts.

- **Dictionaries:** Provide access to grade-appropriate classroom and online dictionaries that include illustrations. Students can also create personal spelling dictionaries with alphabetized lists of words.

Sound-spelling Cards

As students move from kindergarten through grade 2, they are learning letter-sound correspondences through phonics instruction. This includes the different options for how graphemes (letters and letter-combinations) represent the 44 phonemes in spoken English.

Sound-spelling cards include a picture that provides a clue to the pronunciation of a particular sound (phoneme). The most common spelling for that sound is listed beneath the picture, followed by alternative spellings. These cards can be displayed on the classroom wall or in a large pocket chart. When students need support to spell a sound in a word, they find the card associated with that sound and then view the spelling options. Teachers can make their own sound-spelling cards or they are sometimes included with a phonics program. See the examples in Figure 5-4.

Figure 5-4

Linking to Handwriting

Chapter 1 also presented an overview of effective handwriting instruction and the role that handwriting plays as a transcription skill. As students begin adding words, phrases, and sentences to their drawings, it is a good time to emphasize the importance of legibility so readers can access what they are trying to say. This includes making sure that letter formation is clear and aligned to lines on the page, and that there are spaces between words.

Two-Column Take Away: Connect to the Classroom

Add notes in the right column about instructional practices you learned in this chapter.

Drawing	
Labels & Lists	

Linking to Spelling & Handwriting	

Chapter 6
Syntax, Sentences

Sentences are the building blocks for writing. One by one, sentences (oral or written) communicate ideas that add up to make meaning. Teaching students about sentences supports students' reading and their ability to write quality sentences.

Comprehending and Writing Sentences

The ways in which authors express their ideas through sentences significantly affect a reader's ability to access and comprehend those ideas. Sentences that are complex, contain a large number of ideas (also called *propositions*), or have unusual word order will make it difficult for students to comprehend what they are reading, especially students who enter school with limited oral language exposure or for whom English is a second language. In fact, the level of a text's syntax is one predictor of a text's comprehensibility (Snow et al., 2005). Efficient processing of sentence structure is necessary for overall comprehension, and effective readers have knowledge of phrase structures, parts of sentences, and how they work (Scott, 2004).

Sentence knowledge is also essential for student composing (oral or written). As Saddler (2012) explains,

> "Of the many difficulties writers encounter when engaged in the complex act of writing, crafting sentences that accurately convey the intended meaning is particularly challenging... manipulating sentences is both effortful and critical."

Students with limited sentence writing skills across all grade levels tend to write sentences that are shorter, not complex, and represent lower overall quality of ideas. Their sentences also contain less unusual vocabulary and are often filled with grammatical errors. The research guide *Teaching Elementary School Students to Be Effective Writers* (Graham et al., 2012) notes the following about sentences:

> "Students should learn to write strong sentences that convey their intended meaning and engage readers. Teachers should focus sentence-level instruction on sentence construction, encouraging students to consider the meaning and syntax of the sentences they develop. Teachers also should explicitly demonstrate how sentence construction and sentence mechanics, such as punctuation and capitalization, interact to form strong sentences. Beginning in kindergarten, students should develop an understanding of what sentences are and learn the basic principles of capitalization and punctuation. Teachers can use students' oral language skills to support written language skills. As students convey their ideas orally, the teacher can put those ideas in writing while explaining sentences and demonstrating how to write them. In first and second grades, the teacher can model how to identify run-on ideas and break them into shorter sentences. Teachers should explicitly teach the conventions of written English, embedding instruction as much as possible in students' own compositions." (p. 30)

Related State Standards

Common Core language standards #1 and 2 are related to sentence skills in the primary grades. Grade-specific details for these standards are provided in Figure 6-1.

Figure 6-1

#1 **Conventions of English Grammar** *Demonstrate command of the conventions of standard English grammar and usage when writing or speaking.*	**Kindergarten** *Sentence Structure and Meaning* – Demonstrate the ability to produce and expand complete sentences using frequently occurring nouns, pronouns, adjectives, verbs, question words, and prepositions.
	Grade 1 *Sentence Structure and Meaning* a. Produce and expand simple and compound sentences. b. Demonstrate understanding that a question is a type of sentence. c. Use singular and plural nouns with matching verbs in sentences. d. Use verbs in sentences to convey a sense of past, present, and future.
	Grade 2 *Sentence Structure and Meaning* a. Produce and expand complete simple and compound declarative, interrogative, imperative, and exclamatory sentences and choose among sentence types depending on the meaning to be conveyed. b. Use adjectives and adverbs in sentences and choose between them depending on what is to be modified.
#2 **Conventions of Capitalization, Punctuation, Spelling** *Demonstrate command of the conventions of standard English capitalization, punctuation, and spelling when writing.*	**Kindergarten** a. Capitalize the first word in a sentence and the pronoun I. b. Recognize and name end punctuation.
	Grade 1 a. Capitalize dates and the names of people. b. Use end punctuation for sentences. c. Capitalize the names of months and people. d. Use commas in dates and to separate individual words in a series.
	Grade 2 a. Capitalize holidays, product names, and geographic names. b. Use commas in greetings and closings of letters. c. Use an apostrophe to form contractions and frequently occurring possessives.

Syntactic Awareness

Syntax is the study and understanding of grammar – the system and arrangement of words, phrases, and clauses that make up a sentence. To comprehend a sentence, a reader must process, store in working memory, and integrate a variety of syntactic and word meaning information (Paris & Hamilton, 2009).

Syntactic Awareness means having the ability to monitor the relationships among the words in a sentence to understand while reading or composing. Students build syntactic awareness through exposure to oral language when they are young and particularly through exposure to written language that they hear through read aloud or read independently.

Another way to describe syntactic awareness is to think about students as having good *sentence sense* or *having an ear* for sentences that are grammatically incorrect. When they hear or read a sentence that is syntactically incorrect, they can recognize what is wrong and fix it if it is in their own writing.

Children's awareness of the way in which word order affects meaning begins to develop at an early age. Children under the age of two can understand the difference between two sentences in which the subject and predicate are reversed. For example:

Mommy is calling Daddy. Daddy is calling Mommy.

By the time children enter kindergarten, they are able to give the correct answer when asked, "Which sounds better?" for this example:

Swims the turtle. The turtle swims.

The level of syntactic awareness that students bring to kindergarten often depends on how much exposure to oral language they had prior to entering school. Syntactic awareness, especially the ability to comprehend and write academic sentences, should be taught to all students.

Teaching Sentences

As shown in Figure 6-2, the instructional suggestions in this module are organized into two categories: sentence basics (the parts of a sentence and the four kinds of sentences), and instruction to develop syntactic awareness (sentence scrambles, sentence elaboration, and sentence combining).

Figure 6-2

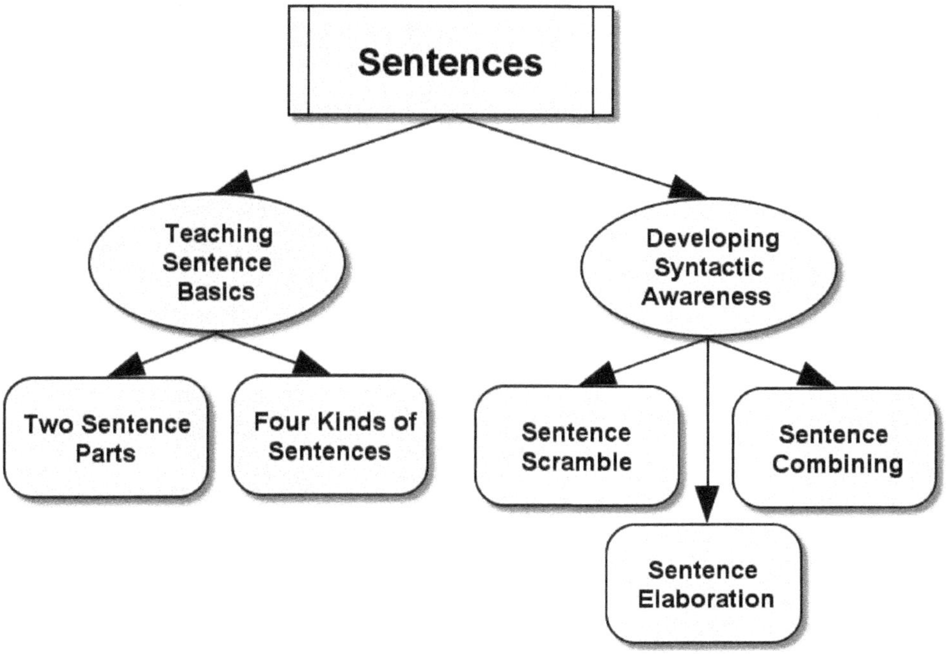

Teaching Sentence Basics

Students need explicit instruction about the basic parts of speech, basic parts of a sentence, the four kinds of sentences, and sentence punctuation. Teaching sentence skills helps all students from kindergarteners who use very simple sentences, to second graders who are writing more sophisticated sentences.

Matching Two Sentence Parts

Students need to learn that every simple, complete sentence must have two parts: a naming part (the subject) and an action part (the predicate). For example:

The turtle	swims.
naming part (subject)	*action part (predicate)*

There are several activities that can develop student awareness of complete sentences that have two parts, as explained in Figure 6-3.

Figure 6-3

Sentence-Part Cards

This activity uses cards with sentence parts that can be joined together to form a sentence. Give students two sets of cards. One set has sentence subjects (the naming part of the sentence) and one set has predicates (the action part of the sentence). When creating card parts, start with short, five- to six-word sentences that are related to texts used in class. Ask students to match subject and predicate cards to create sentences that make sense. This activity can be completed as a whole class activity, during small-group work, in teacher-guided centers, and in independent student centers.

Scaffolds:

- Make the subject cards one color and the predicate cards a different color.
- Include a capital letter for the first word in each subject card.
- Include end punctuation after the last word in each predicate card.

Gradual Release:

- Initially provide card sets for which there is only one correct combination of a subject and predicate.
- Next, provide cards for which a subject can be combined with two different predicates, or vice versa.
- Increase the number of correct combinations that can be made.

Examples:

Subjects	Predicates
Sea turtles	is about Loggerhead turtles.
This book	like to eat baby turtles.
Sea gulls	travel thousands of miles.

Add a Sentence Part
Give students a sentence with a missing subject or predicate. Ask students to complete the sentence by adding words for the missing part. This task is more challenging than matching sentence parts because the students must generate the words themselves. Scaffold this vocabulary challenge by providing a word bank. *Examples:* • The mother turtle _______________. • _______________ finds juicy clams.

Sorting: Sentence or Fragment?
Give students strings of words, some that are complete sentences, and some that are sentence fragments. First ask students to sort them into sentences and fragments. Ask them to explain why they identified some as fragments. Then ask them to add words to the fragments to create a complete sentence. *Examples:* • snaps her beak (fragment) • turtles lay eggs (complete sentence) • claws and beaks (fragment)

<u>*Four Types of Sentences*</u>

Students need to learn that there are four basic types of sentences, and that good writers use all of them to vary the sentences they write. Common Core Language Standard #1 requires students to produce simple and compound *declarative, interrogative, imperative*, and *exclamatory* sentences in response to prompts by the end of grade 1. Figure 6-4 lists the four sentence types, provides information about each, and identifies the related end punctuation marks.

Figure 6-4

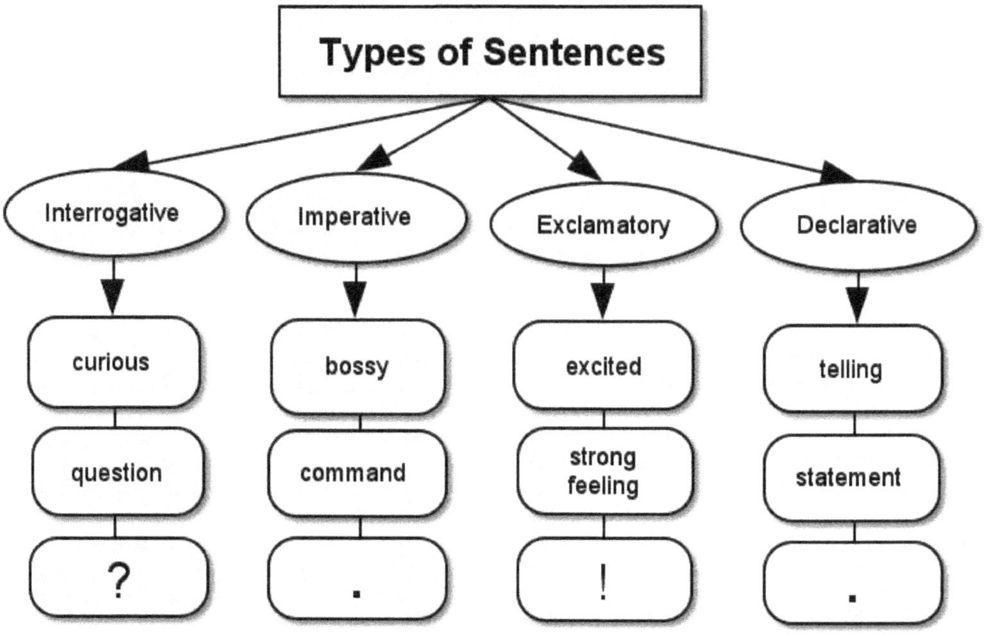

There are several classroom activities for teaching the four sentence types explained below in Figure 6-5 from easiest to most difficult. These activities can be completed as a whole class activity, during small-group work, in teacher-guided centers, and in independent student centers.

Figure 6-5

Activity 1: Sort sentence into sentence types.
Give students examples of the four types of sentences without ending punctuation. Ask them to identity the sentence type and add appropriate end punctuation. *Examples:* • The turtle arrives on the beach *(declarative, period)* • Have you ever seen a sea turtle *(interrogative, question mark)* • If you blink you will miss her *(exclamatory, exclamation mark)* • Look for her in the seaweed jungles *(imperative, period)*

Activity 2: Identify the sentence type and add punctuation.

Give students multiple sentences on separate strips of paper or cards, then ask them to sort them into the four sentence types and add punctuation to each.

Examples:

Statement	*Command*	*Exclaim*	*Question*

Sort the sentences into the four columns:

- Would you like to sit in the bean bag
- Go to the bathroom before lunch
- We have art after morning break
- It is exciting to have a puppy visit our classroom
- Two classmates have birthdays this week
- When is your birthday
- The thunder is scary
- Hang your coat in the closet

Activity 3: Change the sentence

Give students a sample sentence and ask them to turn it into a different kind of sentence. The original sentence can come from text being used in the classroom.

Examples:

- Turn the statement into a question. (?)
  The turtle arrives on the beach.
  When does the turtle arrive on the beach?
- Turn the question into a statement. (.)
  Have you ever seen a sea turtle?
  I saw a sea turtle in Florida last year.
- Turn the question into a command or exclamation. (!)
  Does a sea turtle move quickly in the water?
  Sea turtles race through the water!

Activity 4: Create and write sentences.

Ask students to create one of each type of sentence related to a read aloud book or subject area content. Teachers can provide a word bank as a scaffold.

Activity 5: Find examples.

Ask students to find an example of each type of sentence in samples of mentor text that are being used for reading or read aloud.

Sentence Frames

Writing complete sentences is not an easy task for many primary students. Teachers can provide *sentence frames* as a scaffold to help students generate complete, compound, and complex sentences. Sentence frames are sentences that are missing words. Students add their own words or select words from a word bank. Figure 6-6 shows examples associated with the three types of writing and includes word banks. Figure 6-7 includes additional examples (adapted from Jennings & Haynes, 2002).

Figure 6-6

Sample Sentence Frames

Sample Opinion Sentence Frame **I think a (cat or dog) is the best pet because it _____.** *Word Bank: does tricks, is smart, is cute, has fur*
Sample Informational Sentence Frame **Loggerhead turtles _____ and _____.** *Word Bank: swim, have, dig, disappear, eat*
Sample Narrative Sentence Frame **First the snake_____ and then it _____.** *Word bank: scales, slithers, hides*

Figure 6-7

Sample Sentence Starters

spatial location (where) prepositional phrases	time related (when) prepositional phrases
• _____ is/was *on* _____ • _____ is/was *in* _____ • _____ is/was *at* _____ • _____ is/was *under* _____ • _____ is/was *over* _____ • _____ is/was *above* _____ • _____ is/was *inside* _____ • _____ is/was *outside* • _____ is/was *below* _____ • _____ is/was *between* _____	• *At* sun-up _____ • *In* the afternoon_____ • *On* a cloudy day _____ • *After* school is over _____ • *Before* bedtime _____ • *During* a snack break _____ • *One* summer day _____ • *A long time ago* _____ • *In a few minutes* _____
compound sentence with *and* and *but*	complex sentence with *because*
• The dogs barked and _____ • The dogs barked but _____	• The dogs barked *because* _____
complex sentence with adverbial clauses	
• The dogs barked *as soon as, when, while, until, once, after before, since* _____.	
Source: Jennings, T. & Haynes, C. W. (2002). *From Talking to Writing.* Landmark School Outreach Program.	

Activities to Develop Syntactic Awareness

There are several instructional activities that can help students develop syntactic awareness by providing opportunities to manipulate and add words in sentences: *sentence scramble, sentence elaboration, sentence combining.*

Sentence Scramble

For a sentence scramble activity, students are given a set of words from a sentence that are out of order. They must rearrange the words into a complete sentence that follows standard English grammar. Words cannot be deleted or added.

Examples:

night wait the until hatchlings *The hatchlings wait until night.*

long a flippers turtle her flaps front *A turtle flaps her long front flippers.*

Suggestions for using sentence scrambles with students:

- Use sentences from read aloud books or text read by students.
- Include words recently encountered in phonics or spelling lessons.
- Include newly learned vocabulary terms.
- Use sentences related to everyday classroom experiences, such as the morning school message.
- Use cards with one word per card so students can more easily manipulate the words as they determine the best order for the sentence.
- Introduce sentence scrambles that have just a few words – three or four at the most. Then gradually expand the number of words, as well as the complexity of the sentence structure. Be sure to avoid using too many words that might overwhelm students.

It is also helpful to provide students a set of directions to follow, especially if they will be working at classroom centers with partners, in small groups, or on their own. Figure 6-8 is an example of directions and a handout that students can use to complete a sentence scramble.

Figure 6-8

Sentence Scramble

1	The	Cut out each word.
2	The bird sang.	Put the words in order to make a sentence.
3		Read the sentence to a friend. Does it sound right?
4		Glue the sentence on the line.
5		Write the sentence on the line.
6		Draw a picture that goes with the sentence.

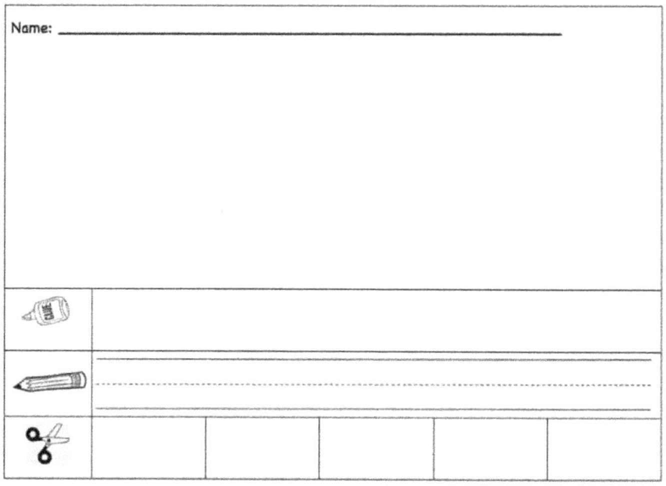

Sentence Elaboration: Use Questions

Young students who have difficulty generating a spoken sentence that is more than a few words have difficulty writing elaborated sentences, but even students who are highly verbal may also have difficulty. Sentence elaboration activities are designed to help students use more words in their sentences. They also help grow syntactic awareness as students add and manipulate words in sentences.

One way to support sentence expansion is to teach students to use question words (*who, what, when, where, why, how*). These were introduced in Chapter 3 and are shown in Figure 6-9. The words *is, did, can, would, will* and *might* have been added as a scaffold to pose a question (e.g., ***Who will*** *go to the store?* ***What did*** *the turtle do?*). Full-size copies of the question cards are in the Appendix.

Figure 6-9

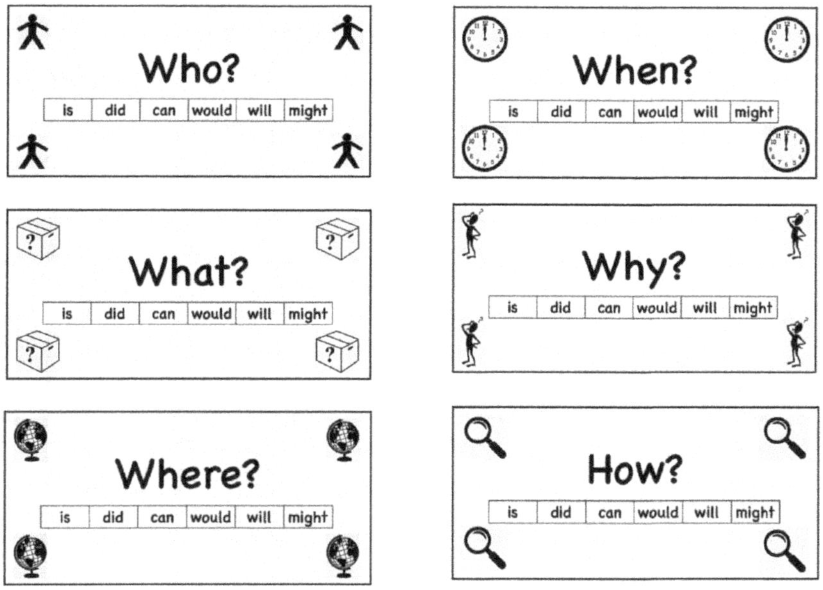

The source for sentence elaboration practice can be a read aloud book, a topic of study in science or social studies, or a picture. The examples in Figure 6-10 start with simple subjects (*the turtle, the Pilgrims*). Then a series of questions are asked to prompt students to expand and elaborate. This activity can be done in whole group with students making suggestions and the teacher writing out the sentences. For older students, this activity can be done in small groups or with partners. Teachers should start by giving students just one or two question words. (Adapted from Adams, 2011)

Figure 6-10

Who? *The turtle*	**Who?** *The Pilgrims*
Did **what?** *The turtle swam.*	Did **What?** *The Pilgrims arrived.*
Where did she swim? *The turtle swam in the ocean.*	**Where** did they arrive? *The Pilgrims arrived at Plymouth Rock.*
Which turtle? *The young turtle swam in the ocean.*	**How** did they arrive? *The Pilgrims arrived by ship at Plymouth Rock.*
What color was she? *The young, green turtle swam in the ocean.*	**When** did they at arrive? *The Pilgrims arrived by ship at Plymouth Rock in 1620.*
Why did she swim in the ocean? *The young, green turtle swam in the ocean in search of food.*	**Why** did they arrive? *The Pilgrims arrived by ship at Plymouth Rock in 1620 to live in a new land.*
When? *Every day the young, green turtle swam in the ocean in search of food.*	

Figure 6-11 shows a template that can be used as a scaffold to help students expand sentences. The teacher provides a simple sentence at the top of the template. Next, students choose two question words to add to the left column, and then add some key words to the right that will be added to the sentence. The expanded sentence is written at the bottom of the template. When students are ready, the teacher can add a third and fourth line for additional questions. Figure 6-12 shows two completed examples.

Figure 6-11

Sentence:	
___________?	
___________?	
Your sentence:	

Figure 6-12

Sentence: *The turtle swims.*	
What?	*green*
How?	*fast*
Your sentence: *The green turtle swims fast.*	

Sentence: *The turtle swims.*	
Where?	*into the seagrass*
When?	*at night*
Why?	*chased by a predator*
Your sentence: *The turtle swims into the seagrass at night because it is chased by a predator.*	

Teach Connecting Words

Students need explicit instruction for using words that will help them connect sentence parts as they expand their sentences. This includes basic conjunctions such as *and, but, yet, so, because, or, when, if.* Teachers should introduce one or two of these words at a time, showing mentor text examples, and modeling how to use them in a sentence. An anchor chart that includes sample sentences such as Figure 6-13 can be posted as a reference in the classroom.

Figure 6-13

and	I went outside, **and** I played in the yard.
but	I want to go outside, **but** it is raining.
yet	I ate a big meal, **yet** I am still hungry.
so	It was sunny, **so** I went outside to play.
because	I went outside **because** it was a nice day.
or	I can play outside **or** inside.
when	I can play outside **when** the rain stops.
if	I can eat more **if** I am hungry.

Introduce Comma

The Common Core language standard for conventions of punctuation expects students in grades 1 and 2 to use commas in dates, to separate individual words in a series, and in greetings and closings of letters. Although the standards do not require students to use commas within longer sentences, teachers can introduce this use to students during activities to elaborate sentences. This includes pointing out how authors use commas in mentor text. Commas can be used in several ways when expanding sentences:

- Use commas to separate clauses when they are joined by coordinating conjunctions such as *and, but, yet, so.*
  - Example: I ate a big meal, yet I am still hungry.
- Use commas after introductory clauses, phrases, or words that come before the main clause.
  - Example: Because it was a nice day, I went outside to play.
- Common introductory words should be followed by a comma.
  - Example: However, I am still hungry.

Provide Word Lists

In order to translate ideas into spoken or written words, students must have sufficient vocabulary. Students who have limited expressive vocabularies tend to use the same, simple words when they speak or write. Teachers can provide word lists as a scaffold from which students select words to use in their sentences that build on their existing vocabulary knowledge. Several examples of word lists are provided in Figure 6-14 (Jennings & Haynes, 2002; Waunakee Community School District, WI). A list of transition words and phrases is available in Chapter 7.

Figure 6-14

Sentence Elaboration Lists

Prepositions

about	beyond	of
above	by	off
across	down	on
after	during	outside
against	or	over
along around	from	through
at	in	to
before	inside	under
below	into	until
between	near	up

Adjective Categories

- Easy: color, size, shape, number
- Six Senses: smell, taste, texture, sounds like, inner feelings
- More Difficult: made of, age, design

Adverb Categories

- how much (greatly, slightly)
- how well (excellently, fairly)
- how fast (quickly, slowly)
- feels like (roughly, smoothly)
- how often (daily, regularly)
- how loud (loudly, quietly)
- inner feelings (happily, sadly)

"When" Categories

- parts of the day (at noon, in the morning)
- weather (during a snowstorm, when it rained)
- units of time (after 5:00, in three hours)

"When" Words

as
when
whenever
while
until
once
after
before
since

Verbs Associated with Inanimate Nouns

(a place, thing, or idea that is not alive: e.g., mountain, house, sky)

leaned	rested
sat	stood
lay	spread
hung	
stretched	

Sensory Words

SOUND WORDS		TOUCH WORDS		TASTE & SMELL WORDS	
blaring	mumbling	bulky	metallic	bitter	oily
booming	noisy	burning	moist	bland	pickled
buzzing	quiet	cool	mushy	burnt	rotten
chattering	ringing	damp	oily	buttery	salty
chiming	rumbling	feathery	pointed	earthy	scented
chirping	scratching	foamy	sandy	fresh	sour
clanging	screaming	fluffy	spongy	fruity	sweet
clicking	screeching	freezing	scratchy	hot	tangy
crunching	singing	furry	sharp	lemony	tasteless
crying	slamming	fuzzy	silky	minty	tough
dripping	shouting	greasy	sticky	moist	vinegary
giggling	silent	gritty	stubby	moldy	
hissing	splashing	hairy	slimy		
honking	squawking	heavy	slippery		
jingling	tinkling	hot	soft		
laughing	thudding	leathery	tangled		
moaning	ticking	lukewarm	thick		
	whispering		velvety		

Sentence Elaboration: Expanding Kernel Sentences
This is an activity similar to using question words, but it is more advanced and provides the opportunity to label parts of speech.

Consider this "popcorn" metaphor for explaining this activity: a single *kernel* of corn is very small, but when energy in the form of heat is added it *blows up* and becomes a larger piece of popcorn. Similarly, students start with a small, *kernel sentence* (a noun and a verb). When they put energy into adding information to the kernel sentence, it also blows up! Students in kindergarten and grade 1 will need the teacher's help to complete this activity, but by grade 2 students will be able to generate expanded sentences on their own or with a partner. Figure 6-15 identifies the steps for expanding a kernel sentence. Figure 6-16 includes an example.

Instructional suggestions:

- Students do not have to follow all the steps – teachers can assign just one or two.
- This activity can be done orally for younger children who are not ready to read and write all the words in their sentences.
- Provide word lists as a scaffold, including the connecting words in Figure 6-13.

Figure 6-15

Expanding Kernel Sentences

- Start with a noun and a verb.
- Elaborate the subject – add articles, adjectives.
  - E.g., color, size, shape, number
- Elaborate the predicate – add adverbs.
  - E.g., time of day, weather, location
- Add a phrase
- Compound the subject.
- Compound the predicate.
- Add a dependent clause to make a complex sentence.
- Combine two sentences into a compound sentence.

Adapted from Jennings & Haynes, 2002

Figure 6-16

BASIC EXPANSION

Kernel Sentence

turtle dives

Elaborate the subject: articles, adjectives

The small, green turtle dives.

Elaborate the predicate: adverbs

The small, green turtle dives quickly.

Add a phrase

The small, green turtle dives quickly into the seaweed.

ADVANCED EXPANSION

Compound the subject.

The small, green turtle and his friend dive quickly into the seaweed.

Compound the predicate.

The small, green turtle and his friend dive and swim quickly into the seaweed.

Add a dependent clause to make a complex sentence.

Because he is frightened, the small, green turtle and his friend dive quickly into the seaweed.

Combine two sentences to make a compound sentence.

Because he is frightened, the small, green turtle and his friend dive quickly into the seaweed, and they hide from predators.

Sentence Combining

Developed in the 1960's (Strong, 1986), sentence combining is an effective method for helping students in elementary grades through college develop syntactic awareness to support comprehension and writing of sentences (Graham & Perin, 2007; Saddler, 2012). Sentence combining provides practice with manipulating and rearranging words in sentences, expanding sentences, and clarifying sentence meaning. Given a set of simple sentences, sentence combining activities require students to apply syntactic knowledge to combine the sentences into a more complex, grammatically correct sentence.

Sentence combining is an alternative approach to more traditional grammar instruction. Studies establishing the effectiveness of sentence combining compared with more traditional grammar instruction found that sentence combining had consistently higher effects on improving sentence writing (Graham & Perin, 2007). Figure 6-17 provides examples.

Figure 6-17

Sentence Combining Examples

Basic Examples

- Birds can eat baby sea turtles. Fish can eat baby sea turtles.
  - *Birds and fish can eat baby sea turtles.*
- The baby turtle swims. The baby turtle dives.
  - *The baby turtle swims and dives.*
- There are six turtle eggs. The turtle eggs are white.
  - *There are six, white turtle eggs.*
- Turtles have shells. The shells are made of bony plates. The shells get bigger as turtles grow.
  - *Turtles have shells made of bony plates that get bigger as they grow.*

Advanced Example

Wildlands are lands.
The lands are public.
The lands are private.
The lands support native ecosystems.
The lands include landscapes.
A grazed rangeland is a landscape.
Active timberland is a landscape.

Combined: *Wildlands are public and private lands that support native ecosystems, including rangeland and timberland landscapes.*

Explain to students that you will help them play with sentences to make them sound better and more interesting, and that this will teach them how to communicate better when they are speaking or writing. Model how two sentences can be combined and think aloud the steps you took to combine the sentences.

Teaching suggestions:

- Start with combining two short, simple sentences. Once students can complete this task independently, lengthen the sentences that are combined, or have them combine three, short sentences.
- Sentence combining can be done orally for younger students who cannot read or write enough words.

- Use sentences related to read aloud books or subject area content.
- Label basic parts of speech (noun, verb, adjective, adverb), but do not make this the focus of the activity.
- Encourage students to explain what they were thinking when they combined sentences.
- Practice sentence combining at least two or three times a week.

Scaffold: Cloze Activity

A *cloze activity* is an activity in which words are removed from sentences for students to fill in using knowledge of syntax and vocabulary. For students who are not yet ready to combine sentences independently, teachers can use a cloze activity that requires students to fill in the blank(s), typically with appropriate connecting words. A word bank can be provided as an additional scaffold. Figure 6-18 includes several examples with a word bank related to the read aloud book *One Tiny Turtle* by Nicola Davies. The examples range from simple to more complex combining tasks.

Figure 6-18

Word Bank and   but   so   however
Turtles swim in water. Turtles dive in water. Turtles swim _____ dive in water.
Fish breathe underwater. Turtles need to come to the surface for air. Fish breathe underwater, _____ turtles need to come to the surface for air.
Coming ashore is very risky for sea turtles. They only nest at night. Coming ashore is very risky for sea turtles, _____ they only nest at night.
Turtle eggs in warm sand can hatch in 6 weeks. If the sand is cool, they can take 3 weeks longer. Turtle eggs in warm sand can hatch in 6 weeks, _____ if the sand is cool, they can take 3 weeks longer.

Revising Sentences

During the REVISE stage of the writing process, teachers can target sentences as a focus for revision feedback. Figure 6-19 is a classroom example of a template that has the sentences from a grade 2 student's paragraph. What revision feedback might you give this student to improve the sentences?

Figure 6-19

Grade 2 Student Sentences

Sentence Number	Number of Words	First 2 Words of the Sentence	End Punctuation
1.	10	**I went** to Disneyland and we went through the desert.	.
2.	3	**I had** fun.	.
3.	5	**I saw** lots of rides.	.
4.	5	**I went** on the Matterhorn.	.
5.	5	**I went** on the Ferris wheel.	.

Figure 6-20 is a blank copy of the template used in the example above. Teachers can use this template to help students evaluate their sentences by listing a student's sentences, along with the number of words in each sentence, and the end punctuation. This template makes it easier for students to notice if they are varying the length of their sentences, varying the beginnings of the sentences, and if they are using all four sentence types.

Figure 6-20

Name____

Sentence Revision Chart

Sentence Number	Number of Words	First 2 Words of the Sentence	End Punctuation
1.			
2.			
3.			
4.			
5.			
6.			

Two-Column Take Away: Connect to the Classroom

Add notes in the right column about instructional practices you learned in this chapter.

Syntactic Awareness	
Sentence Basics: 2 parts, 4 types	

Activities: Sentence Scrambles, Elaboration, Combining	

Chapter 7
Paragraph Writing

As students move from grade 1 to grade 2, the volume of their writing should increase to include multiple sentences that are combined into a paragraph. In second grade, their informational, opinion and narrative writing pieces may include multiple paragraphs.

Paragraph Structure

Students benefit from explicit instruction about paragraph writing to supporting reading comprehension and writing, beginning with the parts that make up the structure of a paragraph. In its most basic form, a paragraph consists of several sentences that support one main idea. In early elementary grades, students are taught that a paragraph has three components: a *topic sentence* that states the main idea, several *supporting sentences* that provide details about the main idea, and a *concluding sentence* that provides some closure. Notice that these components are aligned to expectations in the Common Core standards shown in Chapter 4, Figure 4-9.

The *paragraph hamburger* and *paragraph temple* illustrations in Figure 7-1 are examples of graphics that help students remember these three components of a paragraph.

As students grow older and begin reading different types of text, they learn that the length of a paragraph may vary. They also learn that some paragraphs do not have a stated main idea or a concluding sentence, and that paragraphs may be developed differently depending on their use in opinion, informational, or narrative writing.

Figure 7-1

- **Topic Sentence**
- **Support, Detailed Sentences**
- **Concluding Sentence**

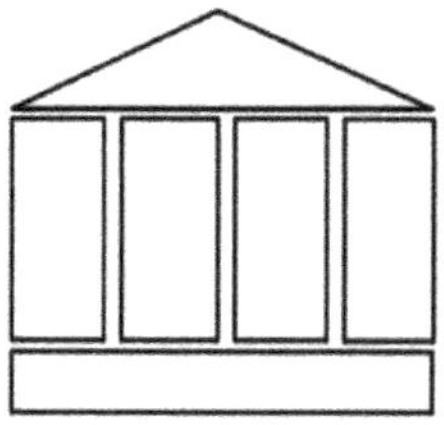

<u>*Reading Paragraphs Like a Writer*</u>

Chapter 2 addressed the value of using mentor text and teaching students to *read like a writer* to learn how authors use writing techniques and text structure. A good way to introduce students to paragraph structure is to share examples of well-structured paragraphs in mentor text, highlighting topic sentences, supporting sentences, and concluding sentences.

Before students can be expected to write topic sentences that state the main idea and add supporting sentences that are related to that main idea, they must first develop main idea skills.

Understanding the difference between main ideas and relevant supporting details begins as a comprehension task. View the Common Core requirements in Figure 7-2 related to main idea for kindergarten through grade 2 that are incorporated into reading standard #2.

Figure 7-2

Common Core Reading Standard #2

#2 Central Ideas, Summary *Determine central ideas or themes of a text and analyze their development; summarize the key supporting details and ideas.*	**Kindergarten** (informational text) With prompting and support, identify the main topic and retell key details of a text.
	Grade 1 (informational text) Identify the main topic and retell key details of a text.
	Grade 2 (informational text) Identify the main topic of a multi-paragraph text as well as the focus of specific paragraphs within the text.

Practice Using Mentor Text

Review the sample paragraphs below in Figure 7-3. What is the main idea of each paragraph? Is the main idea stated as a topic sentence? What are some of the details that support the main idea? Is there a concluding sentence? These are the kinds of questions to ask students as you share mentor text samples.

Figure 7-3

Sample 1 (from an article about lizards):

> Sea lizards hatch from eggs. The female lizard digs a burrow deep in the sand. She lays two to four white eggs in the burrow. She stays near the burrow for about three days, then leaves it. The young hatch after three to four months.

Sample 2 (from *Ibis, A True Whale Story* by John Himmelman):

> Many weeks passed, and Ibis grew very ill. The net in her mouth made it hard for her to eat. And every time she went to the surface for air, the net cut into her tail. But if she didn't get air every half hour, she would die. Winter was coming and it was time for the whales to move to warmer waters. But Ibis felt too weak to make the long journey.

Sample 3 (from *Stellaluna* by Jannell Cannon):

> Stellaluna learned to be like the birds. She stayed awake all day and slept at night. She ate bugs even though they tasted awful. Her bat ways were quickly disappearing. Except for one thing: Stellaluna still liked to sleep hanging by her feet.

Sample 4 (from a page of decodable text):

> Meg and Jim get dressed to sled. They put on snow pants and jackets. They put on mittens and hats too.

Sample 5 (from an informational text about whales):

> A whale breathes through a hole in its head. This is called a blowhole. When a whale dives, it holds its breath. When it comes up, it breathes out. A big spout of spray comes out of its blowhole. Up it goes, high in the air.

Mentor Text Activity: Color Code Paragraph Components

Teachers can use color to reinforce paragraph structure. *Stoplight paragraphs* are color-coded paragraphs that highlight (or underline) sentences using the colors of a stop light. Green is used for topic sentences that tell the main idea, yellow is used for supporting sentences that give details, and red is used for concluding sentences that provide closure. A stoplight visual can be used as a reminder of the order of the colors. Using the sample 2 paragraph in Figure 7-3, students highlight the first sentence green, the last sentence red, and the middle sentences yellow.

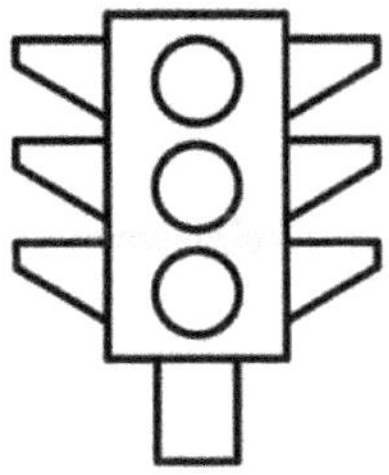

> Many weeks passed, and Ibis grew very ill. The net in her mouth made it hard for her to eat. And every time she went to the surface for air, the net cut into her tail. But if she didn't get air every half hour, she would die. Winter was coming and it was time for the whales to move to warmer waters. But Ibis felt too weak to make the long journey.

To make the activity more challenging, the teacher can write each sentence on a card or sentence strip, and then mix them up. Students identify the topic and concluding sentences, arrange the sentences in order, and then color code them. In the example below, students would rearrange the sentences into a paragraph that begins with sentence *d* (green), ends with sentence *c* (red), and has sentences *a* and *b* in the middle (yellow).

a) In summer she goes to cool seaweed jungles to find clams and shrimp.

b) In winter she goes to turquoise lagoons to munch among corals.

c) She may travel thousands of miles, but she leaves not a trace for you to follow.

d) Loggerhead wanders far and wide in search of food.

Once students are writing their own paragraphs, they can color code their sentences.

Paragraph Activities Using Sample Paragraphs

Figure 7-4 includes several activities for developing an understanding of paragraph structure. The level of difficulty varies among the four activities. Consider how you might differentiate each activity based on the needs of your students. Use well-structured samples of paragraphs from mentor text.

Figure 7-4

Activity 1: Identify the Topic Sentence
For this activity, students are given several sentences out of order from one paragraph. They are asked to determine which sentence is the topic sentence that states the main idea, and which sentences support the main ideas by providing details. Students can read the sentences themselves or the teacher can read them aloud. This may be done as a whole class activity or in small groups. As a scaffold, it may be helpful for students to see the sentences written onto strips that can be manipulated. This enables students to move the topic sentence to the top of the paragraph. The topic sentence has been underlined in the example below. a. She lays two to four white eggs in the burrow. b. She stays near the burrow for about three days, then leaves it. c. <u>Sea lizards hatch from eggs.</u> d. The female lizard digs a burrow deep in the sand. e. The young hatch after three to four months.
Activity 2: Identify the Sentence That Does Not Belong
For this activity, students are given all the sentences from a paragraph, plus one extra sentence that does not belong in the paragraph because the detail is not related to the main idea. They are asked to review each supporting sentence and choose the one that does not belong because the details are not related to the topic sentence. It has been underlined in the example below. a. (topic sentence) A baby turtle lives in a tangle of weeds. b. The weeds are just beneath the surface of the water. c. Just a little fish bite could rip it open, but she is safely hidden in the weeds. d. <u>Grown up Loggerheads have a hard shell.</u> e. She can find tiny crabs and shrimps to eat in the weeds.

Activity 3: Create a Topic Sentence
For this activity, students are given several supporting sentences. They are asked to identify the main idea and then write a topic sentence that states the main idea. A topic sentence for the example below would be *A whale breathes through a hole in its head.* Topic Sentence: ____ This is called a blowhole. When a whale dives, it holds its breath. When it comes up, it breathes out. A big spout of spray comes out of its blowhole. Up it goes, high in the air.

Teaching Paragraph Writing

It is helpful to follow the gradual release of responsibility model for teaching paragraph structure. Follow the suggestions in Figure 7-5.

Figure 7-5

I, We, You for Paragraph Structure

Mentor Text Examples	Teacher Models	Shared Writing	Independent Writing
The teacher shares and deconstructs samples of well-structured paragraphs.	The teacher models how to write a paragraph, using think aloud to explain each part of the paragraph.	Students participate in a shared paragraph writing activity with the teacher, and/or work collaboratively in pairs or small groups to write a paragraph.	Students work independently to write their own paragraph.

During a shared writing activity, the teacher models, thinks aloud, and welcomes responses from students using the following questions as a guide:

- **Topic Sentence:** Who or what are we writing about?
  - *Let me tell my reader what I am writing about.*
- **Supporting Sentences:** What do we want to say about the who or what?
  - *Let me add details for my reader.*
- **Conclusion:** How do we want to end our paragraph?
  - *Let my reader know that I am done.*

The five-day paragraph writing activity detailed in Figure 7-6 is a helpful way to introduce young students to the components of a paragraph. Students build a paragraph over five days, adding one piece at a time. They can work with peers to develop a collaborative paragraph or work independently. The focus for the content of the paragraph can be related to something they are learning in science or social studies, or to a class read aloud book.

Figure 7-6

Five-Day Paragraph Writing Activity

This activity is designed to help students learn how to build a paragraph.

Day 1: Create a topic sentence that includes the main idea of the paragraph.

Day 2: Add a sentence with a relevant detail.

Day 3: Add another sentence with a relevant detail.

Day 4: Add a conclusion.

Day 5: Revise and edit: elaborate on the details or add another sentence, check for spelling and punctuation.

Additional Instructional Suggestions

- Students must have sufficient vocabulary to write paragraphs. Chapter 6 included sample lists of word banks that can be provided to help students who have limited vocabulary.
- Students must have solid sentence writing skills to write paragraphs. Use the sentences in student written paragraphs to practice sentence elaboration and sentence combining.
- Teach paragraph skills during the *Launch* part of a writing lesson. During *Explore*, students practice writing paragraphs and receive feedback from peers or the teachers. The *Land* part of the lesson is a time to share and celebrate paragraph writing.

Paragraph Scaffolds

The *Think and Plan* stage of the writing process is the time to generate ideas or gather information from sources that will be used to write one or more paragraphs. There are two graphic organizers that can be used as scaffolds before students begin writing: *topic webs* and *two column notes.*

Topic Webs as a Pre-Writing Tool

Topic web graphic organizers were introduced in Chapter 4 as a visual scaffold to teach students about text structures for the three types of writing, as shown below in Figure 7-7. The first (*introduction, body, conclusion*) can be used to represent the structure of informational or opinion text. The second (*beginning, middle, end*) can be used to represent the structure of narrative text. In Chapter 4, suggestions were provided for using these graphic organizers to help students recognize the structure of mentor text.

Students can also use a topic web to organize and plan the structure for their own writing that is one or more paragraphs long. When used in this way, the format is flexible – it may include shapes to represent an introduction and conclusion, or it may focus just on body development. Figure 7-8 shows blank templates for topic webs that represent the body of a writing piece. Note that these examples have shapes for 3 main ideas, but the number of shapes can vary depending on how many ideas the students want to include in their writing.

Figure 7-7

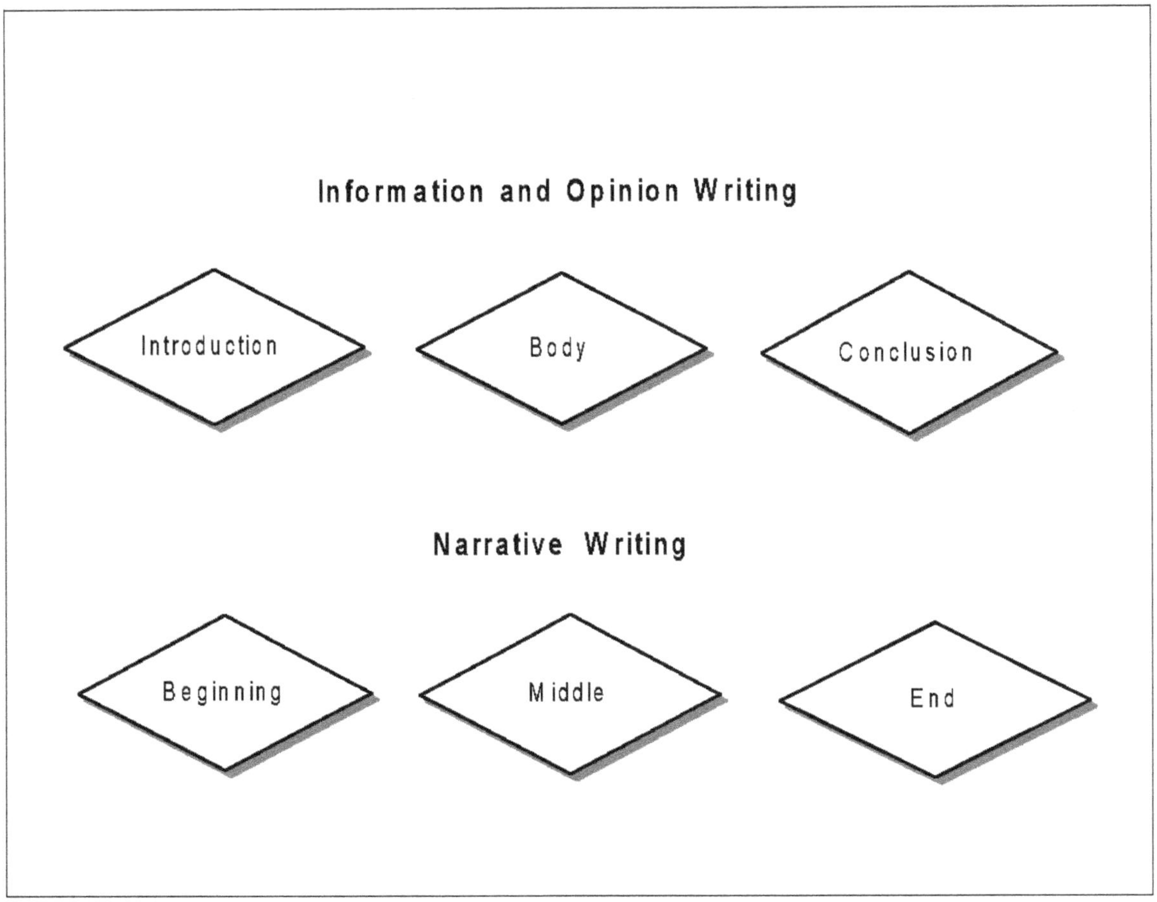

Figure 7-8

Topic web representing body development for multiple paragraphs used in grade 2.

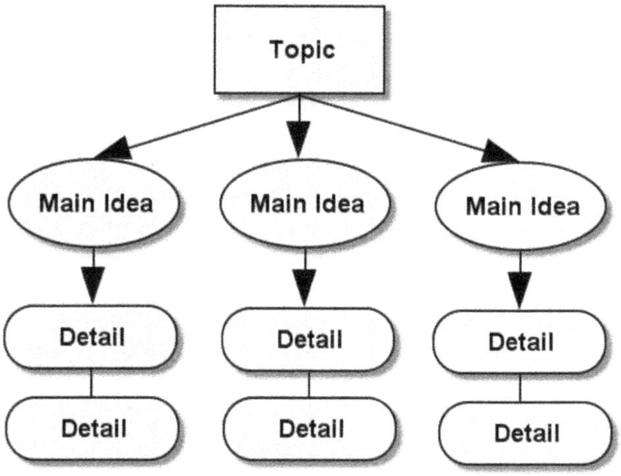

Topic web representing body development for one paragraph used in grades 1 or 2. The first example has space for drawings and single words. The second example has space for words or phrases.

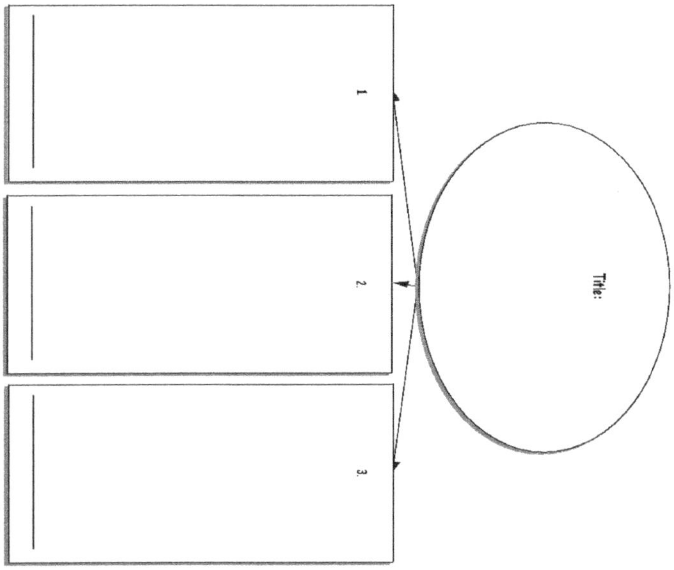

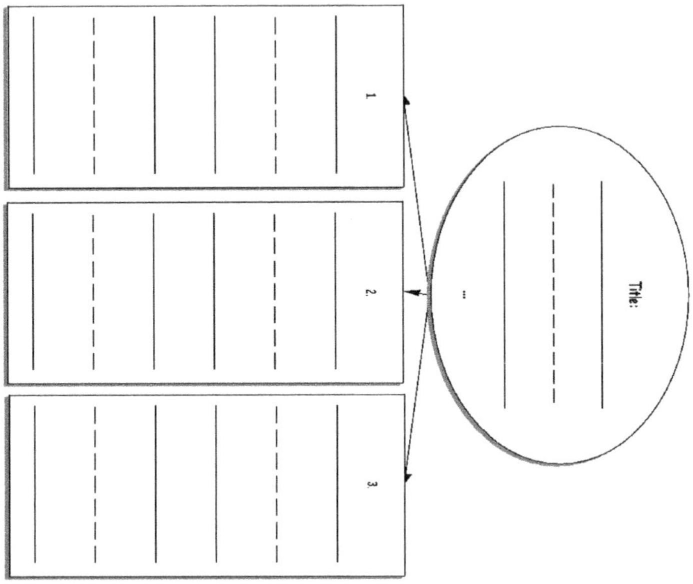

View the student examples of topic webs in Figure 7-9.
Figure 7-9

A topic web to plan a short narrative about a snow day.	
A topic web to plan an informational piece about plants.	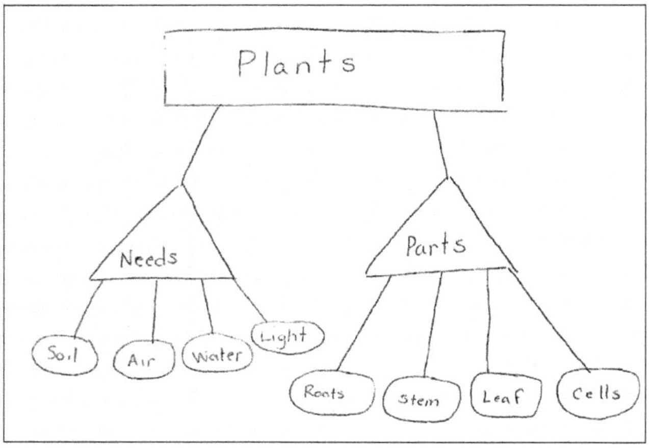

Using pictures in a topic web for a kindergarten informational piece about what to wear in the winter.	
A topic web to plan sentences related to a kindergarten read aloud story.	
A topic web used to plan a grade 1 writing piece about butterflies.	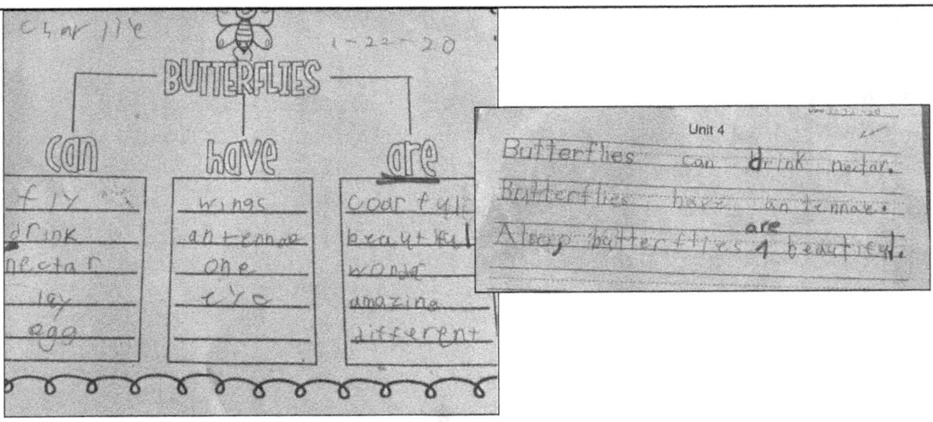

A topic web used to plan a grade 1 writing piece about how the student helps at home, at school, and in the community.	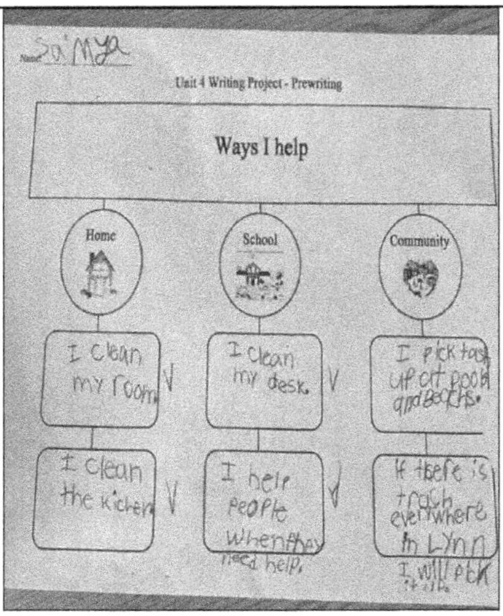 
A topic web used in kindergarten to write about what is needed for school.	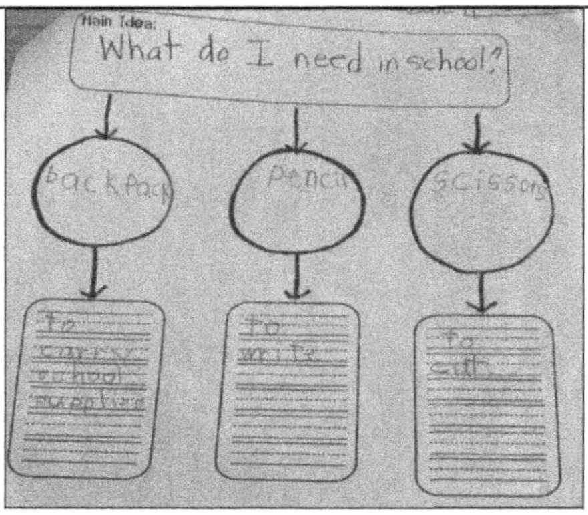 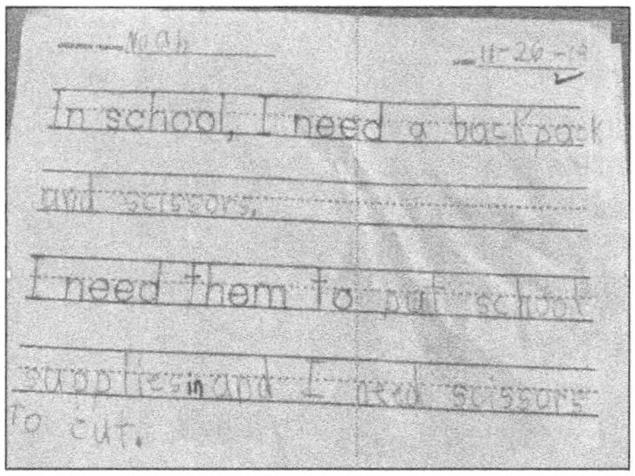
A topic web used to plan a drawing and words about sea turtles.	  

Two Column Notes as a Pre-Writing Tool

Another graphic organizer that can be used at the *Think and Plan* stage of the writing process is *two column notes.* This pre-writing tool allows students to include more detail than a topic web. It is therefore better suited for writing one or more paragraphs. The format consists of two columns, with the right column wider than the left. As shown in Figure 7-10, the left column is used to list the big ideas (i.e., the main topic, main idea, or topic sentence), and the space in the right column is for adding supporting details. Space is provided at the top to write a heading or a topic for the notes.

Figure 7-10

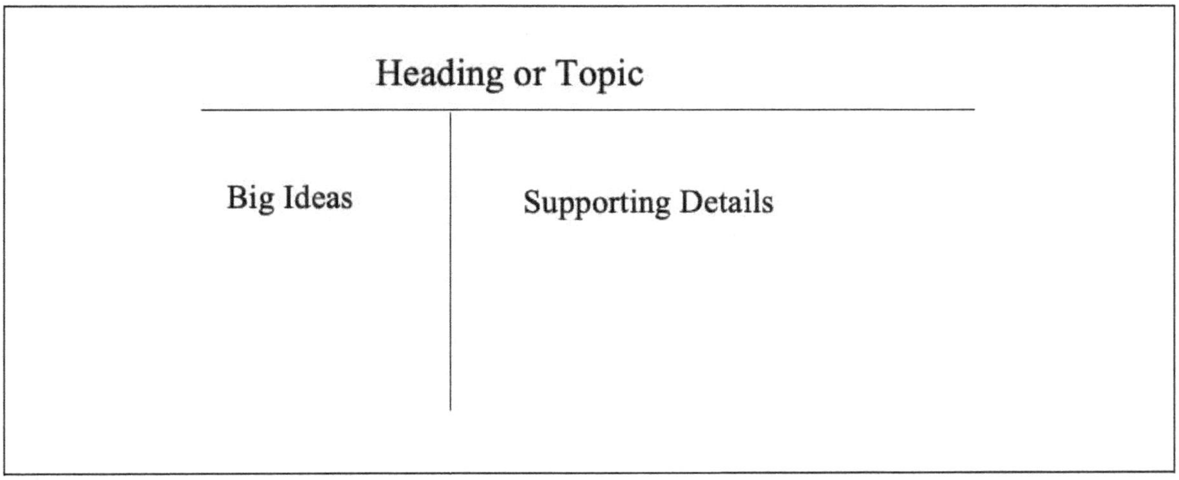

Flexible Templates for Two-Column Notes

The format is flexible and can be used in different configurations based on the writing task and skill levels of students. Figure 7-11 is a generic template that can be used to help students plan a paragraph. Basic and advanced versions of two column templates for informational, opinion, and narrative writing are in the Appendix. Two column notes can also be used for patterns of organization, explained later in this chapter.

Teachers should provide explicit instruction for adding information in both columns. This includes using think aloud as the teacher writes notes, practicing shared note taking, and providing guided practice as students write notes collaboratively with peers or independently. Two column notes are also addressed in Chapter 8 as a tool for gathering information before writing from sources.

Figure 7-11

Name: ______________________________ Date: ________________________

Building a Paragraph

Topic: ____

Topic Sentence	
Detail 1	
Detail 2	
Detail 3	
Conclusion Sentence	

View the student examples of two column notes in Figure 7-12.

Figure 7-12

<table>
<tr>
<td>Notes were developed by the teacher with the whole class. Then students selected details to include in their own writing pieces.</td>
<td>
</td>
</tr>
<tr>
<td>An example of partially completed notes to plan an opinion piece.</td>
<td>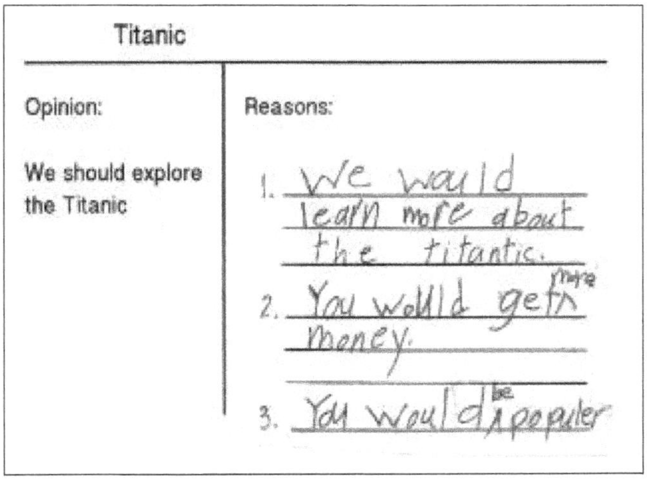
Titanic
Opinion:
We should explore the Titanic
Reasons:
1. We would learn more about the titanic.
2. You wolld get more money.
3. You would be popuiler</td>
</tr>
</table>

A shared writing task: four students collaborated to generate notes about turtles, then collaborated to write the paragraphs.

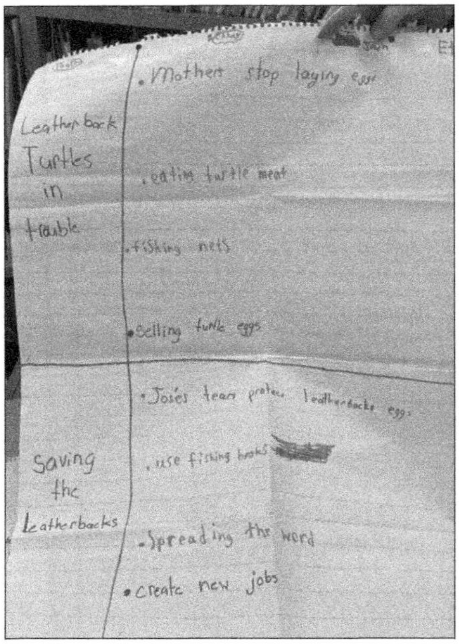

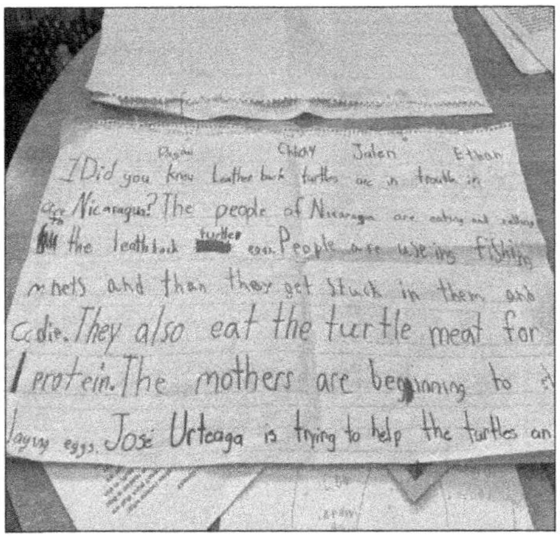

Independent note taking prior to writing a paragraph.

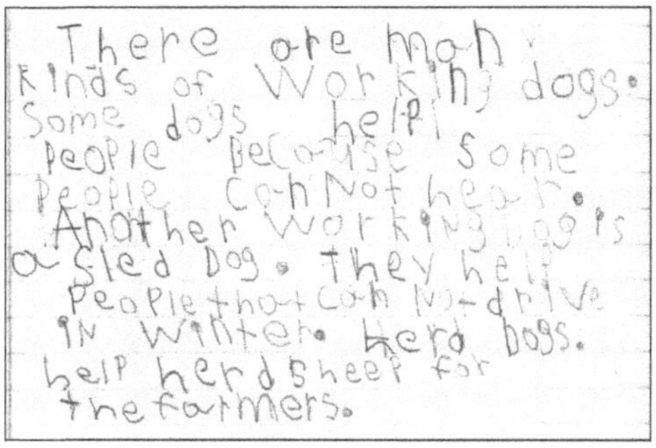

Students added to partially completed notes before writing an informational piece with 3 paragraphs.	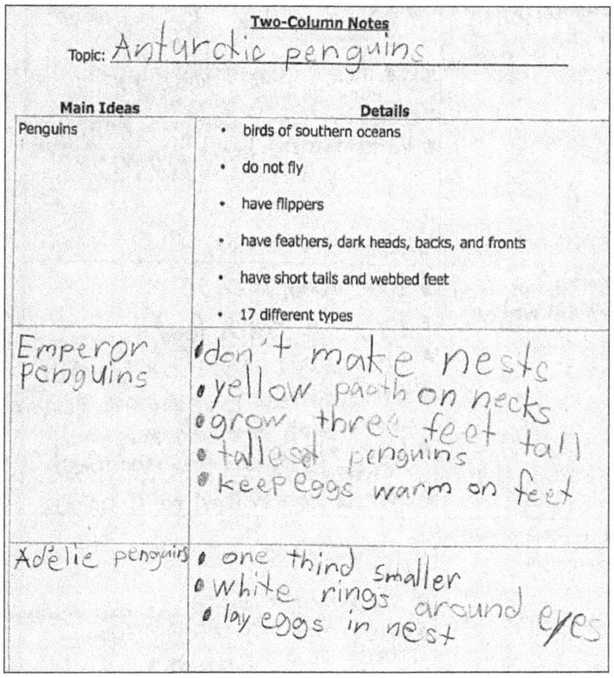 **Two-Column Notes** Topic: Antarctic penguins **Main Ideas** / **Details** Penguins: • birds of southern oceans • do not fly • have flippers • have feathers, dark heads, backs, and fronts • have short tails and webbed feet • 17 different types Emperor penguins: • don't make nests • yellow paoth on necks • grow three feet tall • tallest penguins tall • keep eggs warm on feet Adélie penguins: • one third smaller • white rings around eyes • lay eggs in nest
Students collaborated with peers. Pictures of stages in the butterfly life cycle added on the left column, details added on the right column. Notes were used to write an informational piece.	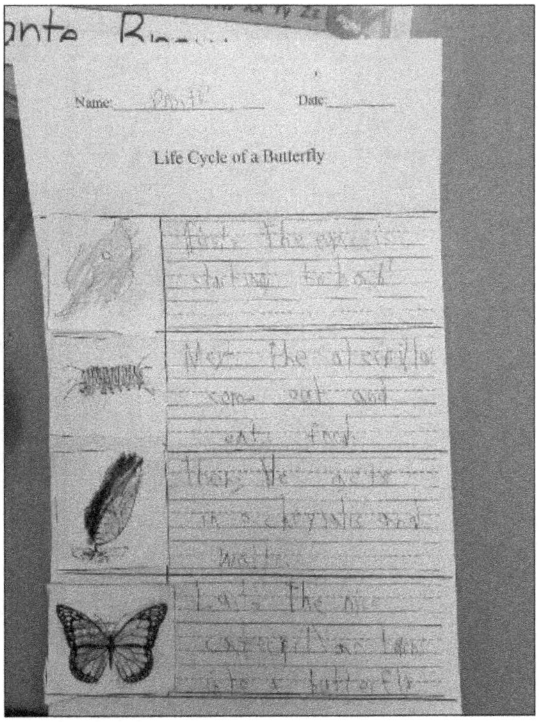

Types of Paragraphs: Patterns of Organization

Patterns of organization are specific structures embedded in text. The most common patterns are *description/explanation*, *sequence* (also called *chronology*), *cause and effect*, *compare and contrast*, and *problem and solution*. Narrative structure often includes *problem and solution* and *cause and effect*, especially related to character and plot development.

When teaching these patterns, the Institute of Education Sciences research guide (Shanahan, 2010) suggests:

- Use familiar ideas or topics and texts that provide clear, easy-to-recognize examples of the structure.
- Use specific graphic organizers to visually represent the structures.
- Advise students that not all texts follow a single structure or only these structures.

Figure 7-13 identifies the five patterns with brief descriptions.

Figure 7-13

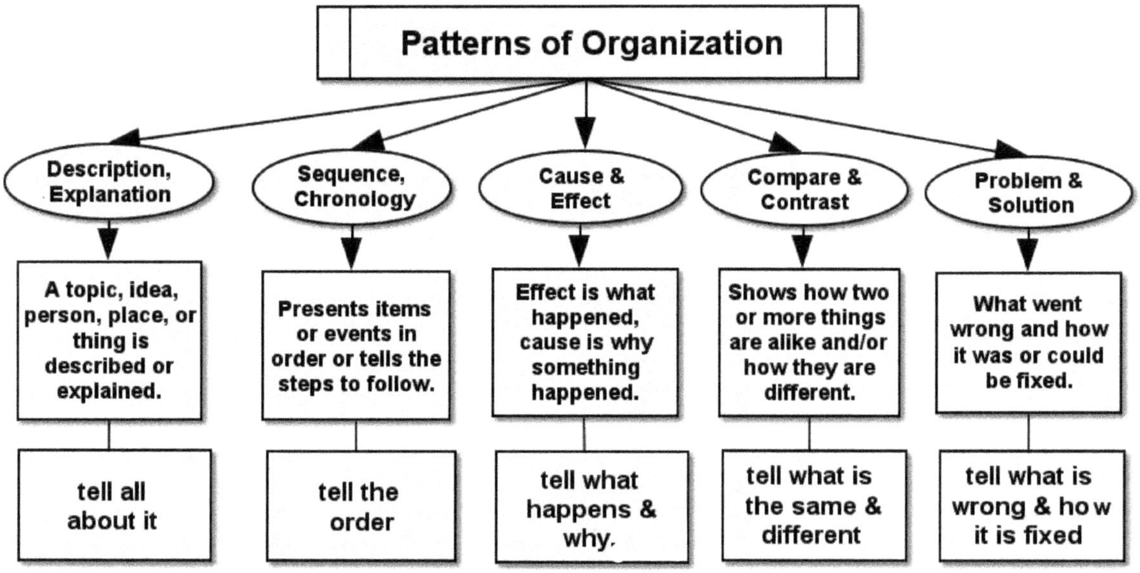

It is best to introduce patterns of organization one at a time, starting with *description/explanation* and *sequence* which are the easiest to write. Begin by showing students paragraph examples from mentor text you are using in class, such as the examples in Figure 7-14.

Figure 7-14

Sample Paragraphs: Patterns of Organization

Description The giant anteater, which is the most common, looks like nothing you've ever seen before. It has a bushy tail and a fat body. It has a tiny mouth, small eyes, and small ears. Its most important body parts are its sharp claws and its long, long tongue. Its tongue is almost two feet long. That's as long as two rulers put together! Source: *Anteaters* by John Jacobs
Sequence/Chronology An anteater looks for ants by smelling the ground. When it finds an ants' nest, the anteater breaks it open with its sharp claws. It puts its long tongue down into the neck. Ants stick to the tongue and the anteater swallows them. The anteater does this over and over very fast until it is full. Source: *Anteaters* by John Jacobs
Cause & Effect With his emergency kit in hand, Scaredy Squirrel watches day after day until one day… A killer bee appears! Scaredy Squirrel jumps in panic knocking his emergency kit out of the tree. This was NOT part of the plan. Scaredy Squirrel jumps to catch his kit. He quickly regrets this idea. The parachute is in the kit. Source: *Scaredy Squirrel* by Melanie Watt
Compare and Contrast Scaredy Squirrel never leaves his nut tree. He'd rather stay in his safe and familiar tree than risk venturing into the unknown. The unknown can be a scary place for a squirrel. Source: *Scaredy Squirrel* by Melanie Watt
Problem and Solution Coming ashore is very risky for sea turtles – they can easily overheat and die. So they only nest at night or in cool weather. Then they get back to the sea as soon as possible. Source: *One Tiny Turtle* by Nicola Davies

Prior to grade 3, most student writing pieces will incorporate just one pattern of organization that is developed across one sentence or one paragraph, such as a description or a sequence. However, more formal writing pieces completed in grade 2 may develop a pattern of organization across multiple paragraphs (e.g., one paragraph for the problem, one for the solution; one paragraph showing similarities, one for differences). A multi-paragraph piece might incorporate more than one pattern (e.g., the first paragraph is a description, the second paragraph shows a sequence, and the next paragraph explains a cause and effect).

Transition Words and Phrases

Transition words and phrases, also called *linking* words, are useful for connecting ideas when speaking, and for connecting sentences and paragraphs when writing. The first three Common Core writing standards require the following related to transitions:

- Opinion Writing: by grade 2, use linking words (e.g., *because, and, also*) to connect opinion and reasons
- Narrative Writing: by grade 2, use temporal words to signal event order
- Informational Writing: by grade 3, use linking words and phrases (e.g., *also, another, and, more, but*) to connect ideas

Students who enter school with significant oral language exposure often use transitions when they speak, and once they start writing, they may include them without prompting. On the other hand, students with limited language skills may not naturally use transitions – these students in particular need explicit instruction for how to use these linking words.

Have students *read like a writer* to learn how to use transitions by sharing examples in mentor text. View some examples in Figure 7-15.

Figure 7-15

Examples of Transitions in Mentor Text

Examples from the read aloud book *One Tiny Turtle* by Nicola Davies:

- "Her shell is hard as armor. **In addition**, her head is tough as a helmet."
- "Inside she lays her eggs, like a hundred squidgy Ping-Pong balls. **Afterward** she covers them with sand to hide her nest from hungry mouths."

Example from *Scholastic News* about recycling plastic bottles:

- **First**, it goes on a truck. **Next**, it goes into a pile. **Then** it gets sorted. **Last**, it gets smashed!

Student writing samples:

- (Grade 2) There are three states of matter. **First** is a solid. It keeps its shape like a bed. **Next** is liquid. It takes the shape of its container. **Last** is a gas, like air.
- (Grade 1) On a snow day the **first thing** I will do is build a snowman. **Then** I will have a snowball fight. **Last** I will build an igloo.
- (Grade 2) Chameleons eat a lot of things. **For example** they eat leaves. They **also** eat bugs. **One example** is spiders. **In addition** they eat berries.

The table in Figure 7-16 lists basic transition words and phrases. A list such as this can be shared with students as a handout or on a classroom anchor chart. Teachers can offer a more basic list with fewer words for students who might be overwhelmed by the full list. A full-page version is included in the Appendix.

Figure 7-16

Transition Words and Phrases

description	looks like, such as
placement	above, across, behind, below, beside, between, in back of, in front of, near, next to, on top of
compare	alike, both, compared to, just like, in common, same as, similar to
contrast	although, but, however, instead of, on the other hand, unlike
sequence	after, at first, before, beginning with, during, earlier, ending with, finally, first, from then on, last, later, next, second, then, third
cause and effect	as a result, because, because of, caused by, for this reason, leads to, that is why, therefore
to add information	also, another, furthermore, in addition
to conclude	in conclusion, in other words, in short, finally, to conclude
to stress a point	above all, in fact, in other words, most important, to repeat
to provide an example	an example, for example, for instance, such as

Two-Column Notes and Writing Templates for Patterns of Organization

Two column notes can be used as a scaffold for planning a writing piece that uses a specific pattern of organization. Templates can be provided that include key words or transitions in the left column. Students add details in the right column. Figure 7-17 is an example of a two column notes for the sequence pattern. Two column templates for all the patterns of organization are in the Appendix.

Another scaffold for patterns of organization is a writing template. As shown in the sequence example in Figure 7-18, a paragraph writing template has space at the beginning for the students to write a topic sentence. Spaces follow for writing supporting sentences, with a transition word or phrase provided as a sentence starter. The templates end with space for a concluding sentence. Writing templates for all the patterns of organization are in the Appendix.

Figure 7-17

Sequence

What I am sequencing:	
First	
Second	
Next	
Then	
Finally	

Figure 7-18

Sequence

Topic sentence:

First:

Next:

Finally:

Concluding sentence:

Two-Column Take Away: Connect to the Classroom

Add notes in the right column about instructional practices you learned in this chapter.

Paragraph Structure Writing Paragraphs	

Paragraph Scaffolds Topic Webs, Two-Column Patterns of Organization, Transitions	

Chapter 8
Writing from Sources

Students engage in critical thinking as they use writing to communicate ideas and information, especially when that writing is based on sources. To put it simply, they are *thinking on paper.* Teaching students how to write about what they are reading, also referred to as *writing from sources,* shows them how to use writing to learn. Usually, source-writing tasks require informational or opinion types of writing, but sometimes a task might require narrative writing, such as asking students to create a different ending to a story they have read.

Writing About Reading: Research

Research has shown that writing related to reading improves writing ability as well as reading skills, and it is an effective tool for enhancing students' learning of content material for all subject areas. As noted in Graham, Harris, and Santangelo's article (2015) summarizing the research-supported practices that can be used to meet Common Core State Standards for elementary grades, "Research supports having students use writing as a tool for learning, including writing about content presented in class and writing about materials read. This results in improved comprehension of such material."

The *Writing to Read* report (Graham & Hebert, 2010) notes that students' comprehension of science, social studies, and language arts texts is improved when they write about what they read, including writing personal reactions, analyzing text, writing summaries and notes, and answering and creating questions about text in writing.

Related State Standards

The Common Core literacy standards place an emphasis on the connection between reading and writing, beginning in kindergarten. For opinion writing, students in kindergarten through grade 2 are required to write opinions based on a book or texts. For informational writing, students in grades 1 and 2 are required to use facts and definitions to develop points about a topic. Most likely they will gather this information from text sources.

Several additional reading and writing standards require students to write about what they are reading or hearing in read aloud text, as listed in Figure 8-1. What do you notice about expectations as students move from kindergarten to grade 3?

Figure 8-1

Writing Standards	
#7 Research Projects *Conduct short as well as more sustained research projects based on focused questions, demonstrating understanding of the subject under investigation.*	**Kindergarten** Participate in shared research and writing projects (e.g., explore a number of books by a favorite author and express opinions about them).
	Grade 1 Participate in shared research and writing projects (e.g., explore a number of "how-to" books on a given topic and use them to write a sequence of instructions).
	Grade 2 Participate in shared research and writing projects (e.g., read a number of books on a single topic to produce a report; record science observations).
	Grade 3 Conduct short research projects that build knowledge about a topic.
#8 Integrate Information *Gather relevant information from multiple print and digital sources, and integrate information.*	**Kindergarten & Grade 1** With guidance and support from adults, recall information from experiences or gather information from provided sources to answer a question.
	Grade 2 Recall information from experiences or gather information from provided sources to answer a question.
	Grade 3 Recall information from experiences or gather information from print and digital sources; take brief notes on sources and sort evidence into provided categories.

<table>
<tr><th colspan="2">Reading Standards</th></tr>
<tr><td rowspan="4">#1 Close Reading

Read closely to determine what the text says explicitly and to make logical inferences from it; cite specific text evidence when writing or speaking to support conclusions drawn from it.</td><td>Kindergarten
With prompting and support, ask and answer questions about key details in a text.</td></tr>
<tr><td>Grade 1
Ask and answer questions about key details in a text.</td></tr>
<tr><td>Grade 2
Ask and answer questions such as who, what, where, when, why and how to demonstrate understanding of key details in a text.</td></tr>
<tr><td>Grade 3
Ask and answer questions to demonstrate understanding of a text, referring explicitly to the text as the basis for the answers.</td></tr>
</table>

Laying the Foundation for Grade 3 Writing Assessment

By the time students are in grade 3, they are expected to have the writing ability and skills to generate multi-paragraph responses to assessment prompts that are based on one or more sources. An important instructional goal in the primary grades is to build the foundational skills that will enable students to meet the demands of grade 3 writing tasks. Review the grade 3 standards above and the following examples of grade 3 assessment tasks and note how the writing responses must include information from sources.

- You have read an article about a bear who is cared for by a wildlife biologist. Write an informational piece describing how Lisa Stewart helps Miracle the bear cub return to the wild. Use examples from the passage in your explanation. (Source: Mississippi Academic Assessment Program)

- Write a multi-paragraph response that explains how cameras were invented to meet people's needs. Include information about how the inventors helped develop the camera. Use information from both passages to support your response. (Source: Ohio English Language Proficiency Assessment)

- Read the passage about a famous American named Benjamin Franklin. Based on the passage, write an essay that explains how Benjamin Franklin helped people. Be sure to use information from the passage to develop your essay. (Source: Massachusetts Comprehensive Assessment System)

While most students in grades 1 and 2 are not developmentally ready to produce the kind of writing responses required to complete these grade 3 examples, they can begin to develop basic skills for writing from sources that lay the foundation for these challenging tasks.

Comprehension and Writing Combined

In order to successfully write an informational or opinion piece based on sources, students must rely on both comprehension and writing skills. At the *think and plan* stage of the writing process, comprehension skills are needed to identify essential information in a source that is relevant to the writing task. Students need explicit instruction for locating relevant information in text sources and saving that information in lists or notes. Once relevant information has been gathered into notes, students continue to use comprehension skills as they review the notes and make decisions about what information will be used in their writing piece, as well as how they will use it. A graphic organizer such as a topic web can help students organize the structure of their writing piece. Once students move to the *write* stage of the writing process, kindergarten students create drawings and words that represent the information from text sources. Students in grades 1 and 2 apply sentence and paragraph skills to integrate information from sources into their writing. At this stage, they also apply their knowledge of patterns of organization and transitions words.

If students are having difficulty completing writing tasks based on sources, it is important to determine if they lack skills related to comprehension, writing, or both.

Extended Writing Tasks

In chapter 2, a distinction was made between *shorter* and *extended* writing tasks. This chapter focuses on two categories of extended writing tasks: written responses to text-dependent prompts, and shared research projects. Both tasks are based on writing from sources.

Written Responses to Text-Dependent Prompts
Writing prompts are questions that teachers pose as the focus for writing from one or more sources. Lists, two column notes, or topic webs can be used at the *think and plan* stage to help students gather and organize relevant information from sources.

Figure 8-2 includes examples of texts for read aloud, along with sample writing prompts. The examples are from a collection of literacy lessons designed to highlight expectations of the Common Core literacy standards developed by *Achieve the Core* and *Student Achievement Partners*.

Review the examples and use them as models to generate your own writing prompts related to read aloud books you use with students.

Figure 8-2

Sample Writing Prompts

Grade Level, Text	Sample Writing Prompt
Grade 2: *A Butterfly is Patient* by Dianna Aston	Pick two characteristics of a butterfly that you think are important. Write a paragraph with at least four sentences describing the characteristics you selected. Use information from the text to explain why your characteristics are important.
Grade 2: *A Drop of Water, A Book of Science and Wonder* by Walter Wick	Use what you have learned about the water cycle to retell a drop of water's experience across our state. Make sure to include as many of the new vocabulary words from the book as you can.
Grade 2: *A Seed is Sleepy* by Dianna Aston	Pick one of these author's claims about seeds. Write 3 to 5 sentences with details that support the claim. – A seed can seem hungry. – A seed can seem sleepy sometimes.
Grade 2: *Around One Cactus* by Anthony D. Fredericks	How do creatures use the saguaro cactus to adapt to their special environment?
Grade 1: *An Elephant Grows Up* by Anastasia Suen	How does the mother elephant help her baby survive? List at least 3 ways.
Grade 1: *Adios Oscar! A Butterfly Fable* by Peter Elwell	How was Oscar able to accomplish his goal of flying to Mexico? Write 2 to 3 sentences.
Grade 1: *All Pigs are Beautiful* by Dick King-Smith	Write two lists. Put 2 to 3 ways that pigs are similar in one list, and 2 to 3 ways that they are different in another list.
Grade 1: *Amelia Bedelia* by Peggy Parish	What did Mr. and Mrs. Rogers learn from working with Amelia Bedelia? Write a paragraph that includes at least two events from the book.
Kindergarten: *Are Trees Alive?* By Debbie Miller	Provide students a drawing of a tree trunk. Ask students to add branches and leaves to the drawing. Then ask them to label parts of the tree that they learned about from the book.
Kindergarten: *Bats* by Gail Gibbons	Draw a picture and write something about one way that bats help people.
Kindergarten: *Cactus Hotel* by Brenda Z. Guiberson	Draw as many pictures as you can that show how desert plants and animals from the book depend on each other. Add words to your pictures.

Instructional Suggestions

Students in the primary grades need explicit instruction, modeling, and guided practice to generate a written response to a prompt. Teachers play an important role in previewing vocabulary and facilitating discussion during read aloud of a text source. At first, the teacher may need to conduct interactive writing lessons to model how to write a response to a prompt, following the suggested model for an interactive writing lesson introduced in Chapter 2 (i.e., *prewrite, compose and share the pen, review, extend*). It is essential to provide opportunities for collaborative, peer discussion during the read aloud and after as students make decisions about what they want to include in their written responses. Oral rehearsal by explaining to others what they want to say sets the stage for student drawing and writing.

Sample Lesson

Figure 8-3 is a sample lesson plan that requires students to write a response to a text-dependent prompt. The example is for the book *Matthew and Tilly* by Rebecca C. Jones (1991). A similar lesson format can be used for a prompt based on any read aloud book. Notice the opportunities for using oral language to process the information and rehearse prior to writing.

Figure 8-3

Sample Lesson Plan

Written Response to a Text Dependent Prompt

Source: *Matthew and Tilly*

Prompt: *Are Matthew and Tilly good friends?*

Task: S*tudents state a response to the prompt, provide at least one reason that supports their opinion, and make a related drawing.*

Materials:

- *word cards that include related pictures for vocabulary preview*
- *category cards (good friends, not good friends) and phrases on strips to cut up and sort*
- *two column note template*
- *sentence starter for written response (I think Matthew and Tilly are/are not good friends because...)*
- *writing template with space for a drawing and sentences*

Vocabulary Preview	**Student Objective:** *I will determine and clarify the meaning of unknown words and phrases.* **From the Text:** *quarrel, got sick of each other, picky, stomped* **Teacher:** Use the word cards to preview unfamiliar vocabulary prior to reading the book to students.
Introduction to the Text and Prompt	**Teacher:** Explain that this is a story of two friends, Matthew and Tilly, who do everything together until one day they "got sick of each other" and had a "quarrel." Present the writing prompt.

<table>
<tr><td>Read Aloud</td><td>Student Objective: I will ask and answer questions to demonstrate an understanding of key, relevant details in a text. I will describe how characters in the story respond to major events and challenges.

Teacher:

Before Reading: Ask students to think about what makes a good friend and what does not. Have them share ideas in pairs and then in whole group. Record ideas on chart paper using interactive writing.

During Reading: Provide opportunities for students to discuss the essential question in the prompt at stopping points throughout the read aloud. Based on student responses, write a list of phrases to represent details that could be used to say that Matthew and Tilly are, or are not, good friends.

After Reading: Review the story. Have students work in pairs or groups of three to sort the responses on the list into two categories: good friends, not good friends (use phrase sorting strips and category cards). Then model how the phrases can be added to two column notes (two categories in the left column, phrases in the right). Ask students to choose an opinion in response to the prompt.</td></tr>
<tr><td>Discussion in Small Groups</td><td>Student Objective: I will participate in a collaborative conversation with my peers.

Teacher: Review the writing prompt. Share the sentence starter as a scaffold (I think Matthew and Tilly are/are not good friends because…). Have students work in small discussion groups to share their opinions using evidence from the text to explain their opinions. This discussion provides oral rehearsal prior to writing.</td></tr>
<tr><td>Writing Task</td><td>Objective: I will write my opinion using text evidence.

Teacher: Ask students to refer to the two column notes or the phrase strips and choose one or more reasons that support their opinion. Ask them to complete the sentence starter to state their opinion and write their reasons in sentences. Ask them to add a drawing before or after they write.

After Writing: Provide an opportunity for students to share and discuss their written responses with peers in small or whole group, and to revise their drawing or writing.</td></tr>
</table>

Shared Research Projects

Recall that Common Core Writing Standard #7 requires students in kindergarten through grade 2 to participate in shared research and writing projects. Teachers can engage students in longer writing projects based on sources that are completed over multiple lessons. Examples of these kinds of tasks include:

- Informational research writing pieces that include multiple pages of drawings (with or without words) or multiple pages of writing (one or more paragraphs per page).
- Multi-page narrative writing pieces that develop a storyline with multiple events and characters, represented through drawings, sentences and/or paragraphs.
- Informational or opinion brochures or display boards.

Individual students can create their own longer writing projects, they can work collaboratively with a partner to create a shared writing piece, or they can contribute one or two pages to a class-wide writing project. These longer writing projects typically include text features such as chapter or section headings and a table of contents. View the classroom examples in Figure 8-4.

Figure 8-4

Research "book" about an animal of choice. Each page has a drawing and information about a different topic (e.g., appearance, diet).			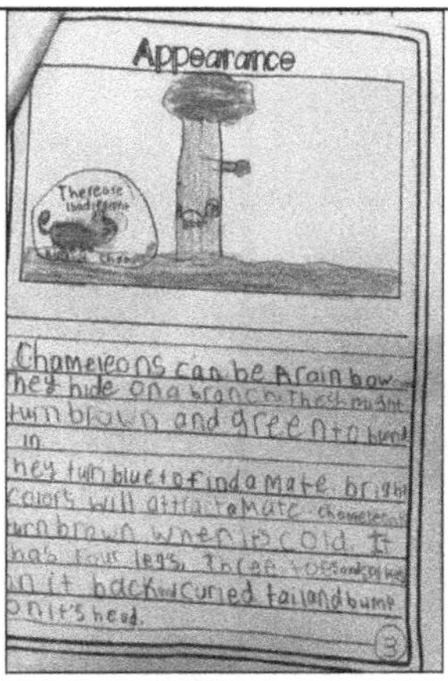
Research "book" about giraffes. Each page has one or more paragraphs that are typed for the "published" book.			

Research posters about a planet of choice. The informational paragraphs are typed and added to drawings on the poster.	 

Task Audience and Purpose (TAP)

Skilled writers learn that it is important to be aware of the *task*, *audience*, and *purpose* for a piece of writing because these elements should influence decisions the writer must make, including (McKensie & Tompkins, 1984):

- Tone of the piece (e.g., objective, critical, apathetic, sincere, skeptical, etc.)
- Language and word choice
- Type of information and level of detail to include in the piece
- How to arrange and present information

Common Core writing standard #4 states that by grade 3, students should "with guidance and support from adults, produce writing in which the development and organization are appropriate to task and purpose." By grade 4, students should "produce clear and coherent writing in which the development and organization are appropriate to task, purpose, and audience." Task, audience, and purpose can be introduced in primary grades so that students are prepared to meet these later requirements.

The Institute of Education Sciences research report (Graham et al., 2012) offers the following recommendations about teaching audience and purpose to elementary students:

> "Writing for different purposes often means writing for different audiences. To help students understand the role of audience in writing, it is important to design writing activities that naturally lend themselves to different audiences. Otherwise, students may view writing in school as writing only for their teacher. When discussing writing purposes,

teachers and students can generate a list of potential audiences for a given writing assignment. Students then can choose the audience that best fits their writing topic. For example, when writing persuasive letters, students could write for parents, friends, companies, or newspapers, depending on their chosen topic. When working on narratives, students could write a fable to read to preschool students. It is important that students' writing is shared with their intended audience.

Students should learn to adjust their tone and word choice to better convey their meaning and suit their audience. To develop this skill, students might write about the same topic for different audiences. For example, students could write a description of their favorite video game for a friend who also plays the game. Then, they could write a description for an adult, such as the school principal, who is unfamiliar with the game. Allowing students to write for a range of audiences enables them to think of writing as an authentic means of communication to accomplish a variety of goals." (p. 21)

As early as kindergarten, young students can begin to understand that writing can be used for different purposes – to convey information or an opinion, to share an experience or story, to provide entertainment, to enhance understanding, and as a means of self- reflection. The introduction of the three major types of text is a good time to introduce the concept of writing with a purpose.

The questions in Figure 8-5 can help students think about the task, audience, and purpose before they write or draw.

Figure 8-5

TAP Questions

Task	**Audience**	**Purpose**
What is your assignment? What are you being asked to do? What form will your writing take?	Who is the audience for the writing piece? Is it your teacher or classmates, or is there another more "authentic" audience? Who will read your piece?	What is the purpose for this writing piece? Is it to inform, convince, or tell a story? How might the audience determine the purpose?

Teacher Planning

The more time teachers put into planning, the easier it is for students to participate in a shared research project. Figure 8-6 suggests questions to consider when planning.

Figure 8-6

What is the task, audience, and purpose?	• related to content area learning • provide choice within the topic

What are the sources?	• consider sources used during a related unit of study
How will the stages of the writing process be supported?	• consider which students will need scaffolds
How will I apply a *Gradual Release of Responsibility*?	• When can I model and use think aloud? • When can I have students collaborate? • Which tasks can students do independently?

About Sources

Sources for shared research projects can be text based, audio, video, or infographics and should be provided by the teacher. Text sources can be read aloud for students who have not developed sufficient reading skills.

Common Core literacy standards emphasize the integration of information from multiple sources for writing from sources. Teachers should build collections of topic-related sources that support subject-area content learning. A text set is a combination of texts that provide students multiple opportunities to hear and discuss new concepts and challenging vocabulary (Neuman & Wright, 2013). A text set can combine narrative and informational texts.

Writing From Sources: Examples

Student ability and skill level to write from sources varies considerably across kindergarten through grade 2, and within each grade level. The last section of this chapter presents four examples of shared research and writing tasks with instructional suggestions and examples. The informational writing task is similar across grades, including the same topic (i.e., *ways to conserve water*) and sources. The difference is in the demands placed on students.

Information About These Examples

- The kindergarten task uses one video source and requires one drawing. The grade 1 task uses two sources (video, text) and requires drawing and sentence writing.
- There are two grade 2 tasks that use the same two sources (video, text). The first requires writing multiple sentences to create a brochure. The second, more challenging task, requires paragraph writing.
- Samples of peer feedback forms and teacher feedback checklists are provided for the two grade 2 tasks. They are customized to address the specific requirements of each task. The teacher feedback checklist is used by the teacher to identify possible areas to provide feedback to students; the full checklist would not be given to students.
- The text source used in all the tasks is included at the end of the chapter.

The task, audience, and purpose for the tasks are stated in Figure 8-7.

Figure 8-7

Task	*Audience*	*Purpose*
to create a drawing/writing piece about water conservation	finished pieces will be shared with parents and adults at back-to-school night	to support content learning in science

Details about each sample task are provided below. The task and instructional details are presented, followed by student samples. The grade 2 examples include sample scaffolds and feedback forms. The goal for sharing these examples is for teachers to see how writing from sources can be taught and practiced across the grades.

Sample Task 1: Kindergarten

TASK

Writing Task:
Make a drawing about one way you can conserve water at home.

Audience:
Copies of the drawing will be given to parents/adults on back-to-school night.

Vocabulary to preview: *environment, conserve, resource, liter, limited*

Requirements:

- Draw a picture related to one of the ways to conserve water from the source.
- Dictate or write words to complete this sentence starter: *One way I can conserve water…*

Source:

- Video: *The Adventures of EcoRilla*

Collaboration:

- Talk with a peer about what you will say and put in your drawing.

INSTRUCTIONAL DETAILS

What skills are needed to complete this task?

- Attention and listening skills to gather information from the video source
- Drawing skills
- Oral sentence generation (for dictation) or sentence writing skills for more advanced students
- Word writing, including spelling and handwriting
- Peer collaboration skills

What happens related to the writing process?

- Think
  - teacher previews vocabulary
  - students watch and listen to the video source
  - students discuss as the teacher scribes information into a list
- Plan
  - teacher and students analyze information gathered from the source
  - students choose one detail for their writing piece
- Write
  - students draw an illustration to reflect their choice, then dictate or write words or a sentence

What ways to conserve water are presented in the video source?

- turn off water when brushing teeth
- take short showers

Student Samples

Left: (dictated, labels added to picture) One way I can conserve the water is by turning off the water when I brush my teeth.

Right: (written) One way I can conserve water is by taking a shorter shower.

Sample Task 2: Grade 1

TASK

Writing Task:
Write about and illustrate at least two ways you can conserve water at home.

Audience:
Copies of the drawing will be given to parents/adults on back-to-school night.

Vocabulary to preview: *precious, resource, gallon, faucet, shortage, environment, conserve, resource, liter*

Requirements:
- Draw a picture for each way you can conserve water at home. Use information from either source.
- You can choose to use this sentence starter: *I can conserve water by ...*

Sources:
- Video: *The Adventures of EcoRilla*
- Text: *Water Wise* (a readers theater text)

Collaboration:
- Talk with a peer to identify the ways to conserve water that you want to use in your writing piece.
- After you finish your drawing, talk with a peer about how you can add more to your drawing and words.

INSTRUCTIONAL DETAILS

What skills are needed to complete this task?
- Attention and listening skills to gather information from the video source and as the teacher reads the text source
- Drawing skills
- Sentence writing skills
- Spelling and handwriting skills
- Peer collaboration skills

What happens related to the writing process?
- Think
  - teacher previews vocabulary
  - students watch and listen to the video source and read aloud of the text source
  - students discuss as the teacher scribes information into a list
- Plan
  - students analyze information gathered from the source
  - students choose at least two details for their writing piece
- Write
  - students draw multiple illustrations to reflect their choices
  - students write sentences about their choices

What ways to conserve water are presented in the video and text sources?

- turn off water when brushing teeth
- take short showers
- use less water in bathtub
- turn off faucets all the way
- don't use yard sprinklers

Student Samples

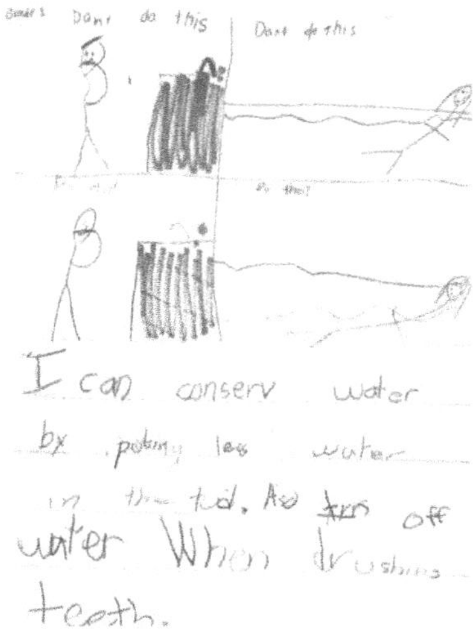

Left: I can conserve water by limiting time in the shower and turn off the water when brushing teeth.

Right: I can conserve water by putting less water in the tub. Also turn off water when brushing teeth.

Sample Task 3: Grade 2

TASK

Writing Task:
Create an informational brochure to explain ways children and adults can conserve water at home.

Audience:
Copies of the brochure will be given to parents/adults on back-to-school night.

Requirements:

- 3-panel brochure format – fold the paper into thirds
- Front Cover (panel 1)
  - Include the title: *Ways Everyone Can Conserve Water*
  - Include an illustration
- Inside Panels
  - Panel 2: write one way children can conserve water with an illustration
  - Panel 3: write one way adults can conserve water with an illustration
  - Panel 4: write one way both children and adults can conserve water with an illustration
  - Panel 5: define the word *conserve*
- Back Cover (panel 6)
  - Provide closure by adding this question: *How will you conserve water?*

Scaffolds:

<u>Two Column Notes Scaffold:</u>

- Use two column notes to organize ways to conserve water.
- Write these 3 main ideas in the left column: *ways children conserve, ways adults conserve, ways both conserve.*
- Add at least one way to conserve water next to each main idea in the right column.

<u>Topic web:</u>

- Use the topic web provided by the teacher to organize the information in the brochure.

Sources:

- Video: *The Adventures of EcoRilla*
- Text: *Water Wise* (a readers theater text)

Collaboration:

- Work with a peer to sort ways to conserve water into the three categories.
- Talk with a peer about what you will put on each page of your brochure.
- After you finish your draft brochure, use the peer feedback form to discuss with a peer how you might add or change something to make the writing piece better.

INSTRUCTIONAL DETAILS

What skills are needed to complete this task?

- Attention and listening skills to gather information from the video source
- Sufficient reading skills to follow along as the teacher reads the text source, OR to read the source independently
- Generation of written sentences
- Spelling and handwriting skills
- Peer collaboration skills

What happens related to the writing process?

- Think
  - students watch and listen to the video source
  - students listen as the teacher reads OR they read the text source independently
  - students discuss as the teacher scribes information into a list OR they write their own list
  - students use two column notes to organize the ways to conserve water
- Plan
  - students analyze information gathered from the sources
  - students choose 3 ways to conserve water that they will include in their brochure
  - students use the topic web to plan how to organize information in the brochure
- Write
  - students write sentences on brochure panels and draw multiple illustrations

What ways to conserve water are presented in the video and text sources?

- turn off water when brushing teeth
- take short showers
- use less water in bathtub
- turn off faucets all the way
- don't use yard sprinklers
- adults: fix leaky faucets
- adults: use broom not a hose to clean walkway
- adults: use a bucket to wash the car

Two Column Notes Scaffold

Ways we can conserve water

Ways children can conserve	*Choose 1 and write or paste here.*
Ways adults can conserve	*Choose 1 and write or paste here.*
Ways both can conserve	*Choose 1 and write or paste here.*

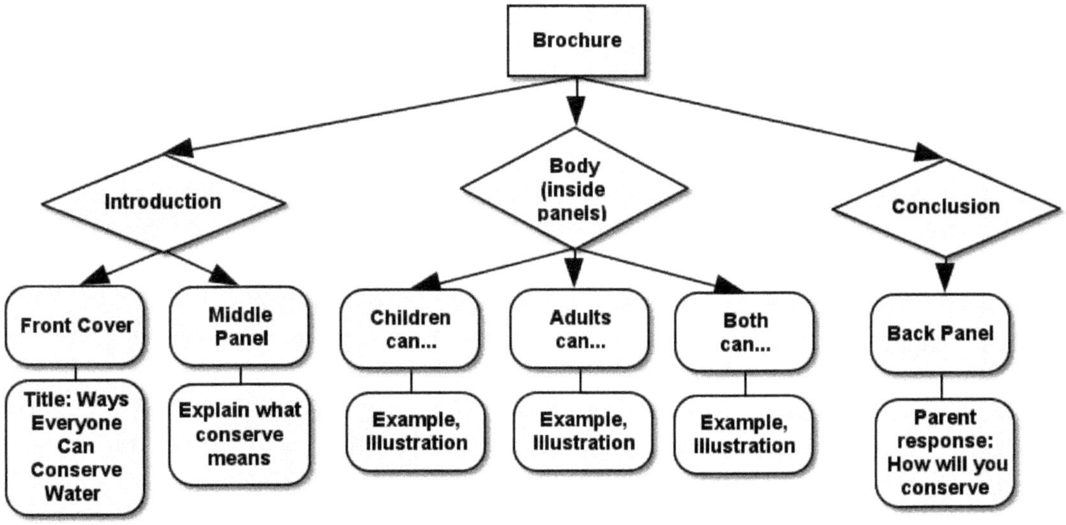

Topic Web Scaffold

Student Sample

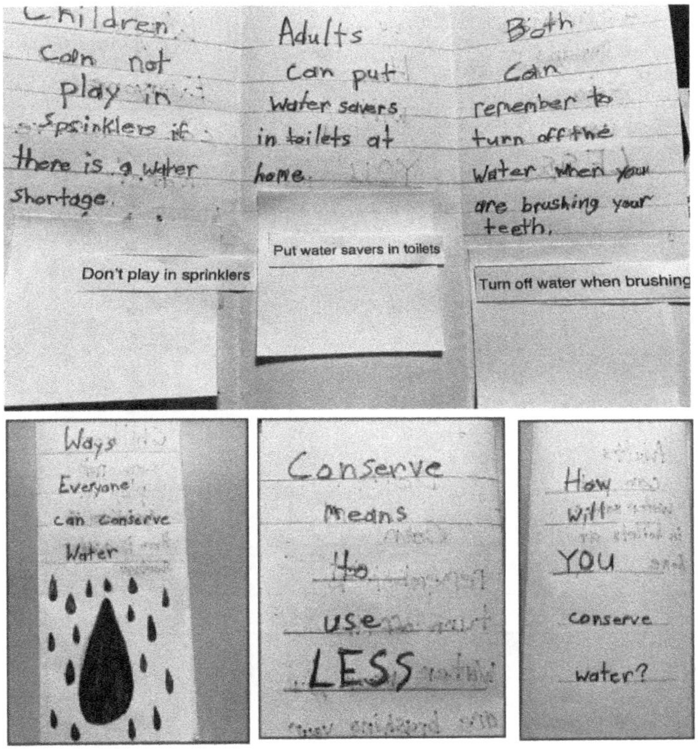

Peer Feedback Form

Your Name: ______________________________

Partner's Name: ______________________________

	0	1	2
Are there 3 ways to conserve water (children, adults, both)?			
Is there a title and picture on the cover?			
Is the word "conserve" defined?			
Does it end with the question?			

Here is how you might make it better:

Teacher Checklist: Ways to Conserve Water

Front Panel	Excellent	Getting There	Not Yet
Is there a title?			
Is there an illustration?			
Inside Panels			
2nd Panel: Is there one way children can conserve water with an illustration?			
3rd Panel: Is there a different way an adult can conserve water with an illustration?			
4th Panel: Is there a way both children and adults can conserve water with an illustration?			
5th Panel: Is the word "conserve" explained?			
Back Panel			
Has this question been included: *How can we both conserve water?*			

Conventions	Yes	No
Are there any capitalization or punctuation mistakes?		
Are there any spelling mistakes?		
Are the sentences complete?		

Additional Comments or Suggestions:

____

____

____

____

Teacher Feedback Checklist

Sample Task 3: Grade 2 (More Challenging)

TASK

Sample Task: Grade 2 (More Challenging)

Writing Task:
Write a report about ways to conserve water at home. Organize at least four ways to conserve water into at least 2 paragraphs.

Audience:
Copies of the reports will be given to parents/adults on back-to-school night.

Requirements:

THINK & PLAN
- Select at least four ways to conserve water using information from both sources.
- Use two column notes to organize the ways to conserve water into at least two paragraphs.
  - Write the main idea for each paragraph in the left column.
  - Add the details from the sources in the right column.
  - You do not have to write full sentences in your notes.

WRITE
- Include an introduction sentence at the start of the report that tells the reader the topic of the report.
- Start each paragraph with a topic sentence. Then add supporting sentences that explain ways to conserve water.
- Include a concluding sentence at the end of the report that provides some closure.

REVISE
- Read your paragraphs and make sure that what you want to say will be clear to the reader.
- Add some transition words or phrases.
- Make sure you write complete sentences.
- Check for spelling and punctuation.

Scaffolds:
- Use two-column notes to organize ways to conserve water.
- Refer to the list of transitions.

Sources:
- Video: *The Adventures of EcoRilla*
- Text: *Water Wise* (a readers theatre text)

Collaboration:
- Talk with a peer about how you might organize your ways to conserve water into two-column notes.
- Talk with a peer to write introduction and conclusion sentences for your writing piece.

- After you finish your report, use the peer feedback form to discuss with a peer how you might add or change something to make the writing piece better.

INSTRUCTIONAL DETAILS

What skills are needed to complete this task?

- Attention and listening skills to gather information from the video
- Sufficient reading skills to read the source independently
- Sentence and paragraph skills
- Spelling and handwriting skills
- Peer collaboration skills

What happens related to the writing process?

- Think
  - students watch and listen to the video source
  - students read the text source
  - students discuss as the teacher scribes information into a list OR they write their own list
  - students use two column notes to organize the ways to conserve water
  - students analyze information gathered from the sources and determine at least two categories for ways to conserve water that will form the basis for their paragraphs
  - students identify at least 4 ways to conserve water to include in their paragraphs
- Plan
  - students use the topic web to plan how to organize their writing piece
- Write
  - students write introduction and conclusion sentences
  - students write paragraphs

What ways to conserve water are presented in the video and text sources?

- turn off water when brushing teeth
- take short showers
- use less water in bathtub
- turn off faucets all the way
- don't use yard sprinklers
- adults: fix leaky faucets
- adults: use broom not a hose to clean walkway
- adults: use a bucket to wash the car

Two-Column Notes Scaffold

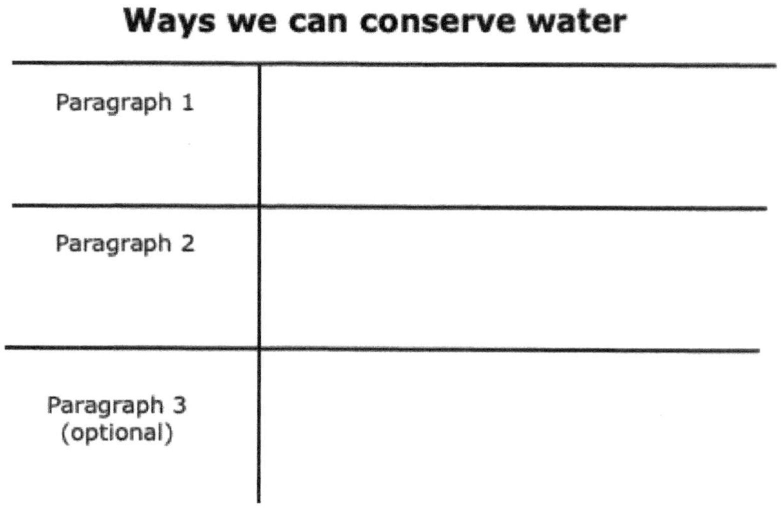

Topic Web Scaffold

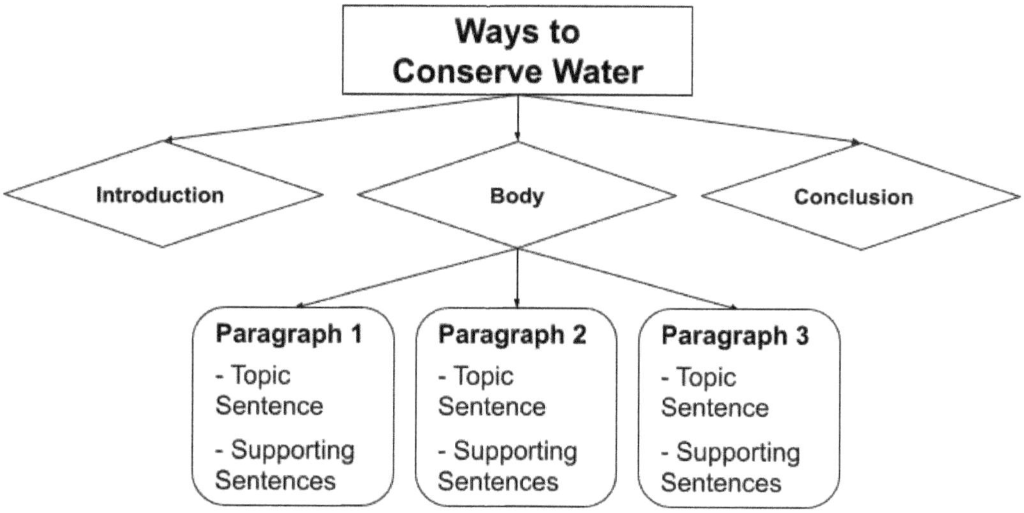

Peer Feedback Form

Your Name: ____

Partner's Name: ____

	No	Yes
Is there an introduction?		
Are there at least 2 paragraphs?		
Does each paragraph start with a topic sentence?		
Are there at least 4 ways to conserve water?		
Is there a conclusion?		
Here is how you might make it better:		

	Excellent	Getting There	Not Yet
Is there an introduction?			
Is there a conclusion?			
Are there at least two paragraphs?			
Are there at least four ways to conserve water?			
Do the paragraphs start with topic sentences?			
Are all the sentences complete?			
Were transition words or phrases used?			
Is the information accurate and relevant?			

Conventions	Yes	No
Are there any capitalization or punctuation mistakes?		
Are there any spelling mistakes?		

Teacher Feedback Checklist

Text Source

Adapted from: *Water Wise: All About Water Conservation* by Lisa Blau	
PART 1 (used with all examples)	
Water Expert #1	Good morning! We are here to tell you all about the earth's most precious resource... water!
Water Expert #2	Every form of life needs water to live.
Water Expert #3	A tiny fish needs water...
Water Expert #1	A tall tree needs water...
Water Expert #2	Everyone needs... water!!
Water Expert #3	We know that water is precious so we must find ways to save all the water we can.
Water Expert #1	Now, you might be thinking... but I'm just a kid. What can I do to save water?
Water Expert #2	Well, we're here to tell you... plenty!
Water Expert #3	If each person in your home turns off the running water when they brush their teeth they can save 35 gallons of water in one week!
Water Expert #1	Don't use more water than you really need. You really don't need to fill your bathtub up all the way when you take a bath.
Water Expert #2	If you take a shorter shower... you can save 75 gallons of water in one week!
Water Expert #3	Everyone in your home should make sure that the faucet is turned off all the way. Don't leave it dripping...every drop counts, you know!
Water Expert #1	Never play in sprinklers if your town is having a water shortage. Sure, it's tons of fun, but you will use over 10 gallons of water in only one minute!
PART 2 (used only with the grade 2 examples)	
Water Expert #2	What are some things that grownups in your home can do to save water?
Water Expert #3	They can fix leaky faucets and put water savers in the toilets. A plastic bottle filled with pebbles with do the job!
Water Expert #1	Grownups should use a broom… not the hose, to clean a driveway or sidewalk.
Water Expert #2	How can they save water when they wash the car? It's easy, just use a bucket and only use the hose to rinse it off.
All	We hope that you will be water wise and save lots of water. We know you can do it! The End.
Source: Achieve the Core	

Two-Column Take Away: Connect to the Classroom

Add notes in the right column about instructional practices you learned in this chapter.

Writing Prompts About Content	
Shared Research & Writing Projects	

Writing from Sources: Four Examples	

Appendix

COMMON CORE STATE STANDARDS RELATED TO WRITING

Common Core Writing Standards

#1 Argument/Opinion *Write arguments to support claims in an analysis of substantive topics or texts, using valid reasoning and relevant and sufficient evidence.*	**Kindergarten** Use a combination of drawing, dictating, and writing to compose opinion pieces in which they tell a reader the topic or the name of the book they are writing about and state an opinion or preference about the topic or book.
	Grade 1 Write opinion pieces in which they introduce the topic or name the book they are writing about, state an opinion, supply a reason for the opinion, and provide some sense of closure.
	Grade 2 Write opinion pieces in which they introduce the topic or book they are writing about, state an opinion, supply reasons that support the opinion, use linking words (e.g., *because, and, also*) to connect opinion and reasons, and provide a concluding statement or section.
	Grade 3 Write opinion pieces on topics or texts, supporting a point of view with reasons. a. Introduce the topic or text they are writing about, state an opinion, and create an organizational structure that lists reasons. b. Provide reasons that support the opinion. c. Use linking words and phrases (e.g., *because, therefore, since, for example)* to connect opinions and reasons. d. Provide a concluding statement or section.
#2 Informational *Write informative/explanatory texts to examine and convey complex ideas and information clearly and accurately through the effective selection, organization, and analysis of content.*	**Kindergarten** Use a combination of drawing, dictating, and writing to compose informative/explanatory texts in which they name what they are writing about and supply some information about the topic.
	Grade 1 Write informative/explanatory texts in which they name a topic, supply some facts about the topic, and provide some sense of closure.
	Grade 2 Write informative/explanatory texts in which they introduce a topic, use facts and definitions to develop points, and provide a concluding statement or section.
	Grade 3 Write informative/explanatory texts to examine a topic and convey ideas and information clearly. a. Introduce a topic and group related information together; include illustrations when useful to aiding comprehension. b. Develop the topic with facts, definitions, and details. c. Use linking words and phrases (e.g., *also , another, and, more, but*) to connect ideas. d. Provide a concluding statement or section.

#3 Narrative *Write narratives to develop real or imagined experiences or events using effective technique, well-chosen details, and well-structured event sequence.*	**Kindergarten** Use a combination of drawing, dictating, and writing to narrate a single event or several loosely linked events, tell about the events in the order in which they occurred, and provide a reaction to what happened.
	Grade 1 Write narrative in which they recount two or more appropriately sequenced events, include some details regarding what happened, use temporal words to signal event order, and provide some sense of closure.
	Grade 2 Write narratives in which they recount a well-elaborated event or short sequence of events, include details to describe actions, thoughts, and feelings, use temporal words to signal event order, and provide a sense of closure.
	Grade 3 Write narratives to develop real or imagined experiences or events using effective technique, descriptive details, and clear event sequences. a. Establish a situation and introduce a narrator and/or characters; organize an event sequence that unfolds naturally. b. Use dialogue and descriptions of actions, thoughts, and feelings to develop experiences and events or show the response of characters to situations. c. Use temporal words and phrases to signal event order. d. Provide a sense of closure.
#4 Task, Purpose, Audience *Produce clear and coherent writing in which the development, organization, and style are appropriate to task, purpose, audience.*	**Begins in Grade 3** With guidance and support from adults, produce writing in which the development and organization are appropriate to task and purpose.
#5 Writing Process *Develop and strengthen writing as needed by planning, revising, editing, rewriting, or trying a new approach.*	**Kindergarten** With guidance and support from adults, respond to questions and suggestions from peers and add details to strengthen writing as needed.
	Grade 1 With guidance and support from adults, focus on a topic, respond to questions and suggestions from peers, and add details to strengthen writing as needed.
	Grade 2 With guidance and support from adults and peers, focus on a topic and strengthen writing as needed by revising and editing.
	Grade 3 With guidance and support from peers and adults, develop and strengthen writing as needed by planning, revising, and editing .

#6 Using Technology *Use technology, including the Internet, to produce and publish writing and to interact and collaborate with others.*	**Kindergarten** With guidance and support from adults, explore a variety of digital tools to produce and publish writing, including in collaboration with peers.
	Grades 1 & 2 With guidance and support from adults, use a variety of digital tools to produce and publish writing, including in collaboration with peers.
	Grade 3 With guidance and support from adults, use technology to produce and publish writing (using keyboarding skills) as well as to interact and collaborate with others.
#7 Research Projects *Conduct short as well as more sustained research projects based on focused questions, demonstrating understanding of the subject under investigation.*	**Kindergarten** Participate in shared research and writing projects (e.g., explore the number of books by a favorite author and express opinions about them).
	Grade 1 Participate in shared research and writing projects (e.g., explore a number of "how-to" books on a given topic and use them to write a sequence of instructions).
	Grade 2 Participate in shared research and writing projects (e.g., read a number of books on a single topic to produce a report; record science observations).
	Grade 3 Conduct short research projects that build knowledge about a topic.
#8 Integrate Information *Gather relevant information from multiple print and digital sources, and integrate information.*	**Kindergarten & Grade 1** With guidance and support from adults, recall information from experiences or gather information from provided sources to answer a question.
	Grade 2 Recall information from experiences or gather information from experiences of gather information from provided sources to answer a question.
	Grade 3 Recall information from experiences or gather information from print and digital sources; take brief notes on sources and sort evidence into provided categories.
#9 Draw Evidence from Text *Draw evidence from literary or informational texts to support analysis, reflection, and research.*	**Begins in Grade 4**

#10 Write Routinely *Write routinely over extended time frames (time for research, reflection, and revision) and shorter time frames (a single sitting or a day or two) for a range of tasks, purposes, and audiences.*	**Begins in Grade 3** Write routinely over extended time frames (time for research, reflection, and revision) and shorter time frames (a single sitting or a day or two) for a range of discipline-specific tasks, purposes, and audiences.

Common Core Standards Reading Comprehension Related to Writing

#1 Close Reading *Read closely to determine what the text says explicitly and to make logical inferences from it; cite specific text evidence when writing or speaking to support conclusions drawn from it.*	**Kindergarten** With prompting and support, ask and answer questions about key details in a text.
	Grade 1 Ask and answer questions about key details in a text.
	Grade 2 Ask and answer questions such as who, what, where, when, why and how to demonstrate understanding of key details in a text.
	Grade 3 Ask and answer questions to demonstrate understanding of a text, referring explicitly to the text as the basis for the answers.
#2 Central Ideas, Summary *Determine central ideas or themes of a text and analyze their development; summarize the key supporting details and ideas.*	**Kindergarten** (informational text) With prompting and support, identify the main topic and retell key details of a text. (narrative text) With prompting and support, retell familiar stories, including key details.
	Grade 1 (informational text) Identify the main topic and retell key details of a text. (narrative text) Retell stories, including key details and demonstrate understanding of their central message or lesson.
	Grade 2 (informational text)Identify the main topic of a multi-paragraph text as well as the focus of specific paragraphs within the text. (narrative text) Recount stories, including fables an folktales from diverse cultures, and determine their central message, lesson, or moral.
	Grade 3 (informational text) Determine the main idea of a text; recount the key details and explain how they support the main idea.

	(narrative text) Recount stories, including fables, folktales, and myths from diverse cultures; determine the central message, lesson, or moral and explain how it is conveyed through key details in the text.
#5 Text Analyzation *Analyze the structure of texts, including how specific sentences, paragraphs and larger portions of the text (e.g. a section, chapter, scene or stanza) relate to each other and the whole.*	**Kindergarten** (informational text) Identify the front cover, back cover and title page of a book. (narrative text) Recognize common types of texts (e.g., storybooks, poems).
	Grade 1 (informational text) Know and use various text features (e.g., headings, tables of contents, glossaries, electronic menus, icons) to locate key facts or information in a text. (narrative text) Explain major differences between books that tell stories and books that give information, drawing on a wide reading of a range of text types.
	Grade 2 (informational text) Know and use various text features (e.g., captions, bold print, subheadings, glossaries, indexes, electronic menus, icons) to locate key facts or information in a text efficiently. (narrative text) Describe the overall structure of a story, including describing how the beginning introduces the story and the ending concludes the action.
	Grade 3 (informational text) Use text features and search tools (e.g., key words, sidebars, hyperlinks) to locate information relevant to a given topic efficiently. (narrative text) Refer to parts of stories, dramas, and poems when writing or speaking about a text, using terms such as chapter, scene and stanza; describe how each successive part builds on earlier sections.

Common Core Language Standards Related to Writing

#1 **Conventions of English Grammar** *Demonstrate command of the conventions of standard English grammar and usage when writing or speaking.*	**Kindergarten** *Sentence Structure and Meaning* – Demonstrate the ability to produce and expand complete sentences using frequently occurring nouns, pronouns, adjectives, verbs, question words, and prepositions. – Form questions that seek additional information, rather than a simple *yes/no* answer. *Word Usage* – Form regular plural nouns orally by adding /s/ or /es/.
	Grade 1

	Sentence Structure and Meaning – Produce and expand simple and compound sentences. – Demonstrate understanding that a question is a type of sentence. – Use singular and plural nouns with matching verbs in sentences. – Use verbs in sentences to convey a sense of past, present, and future. *Word Usage* – Use common, proper, and possessive nouns. – Use personal, possessive, and indefinite pronouns. – Use frequently occurring prepositions, adjectives, adverbs, conjunctions, and articles.
	Grade 2 *Sentence Structure and Meaning* – Produce and expand complete simple and compound declarative, interrogative, imperative, and exclamatory sentences and choose among sentence types depending on the meaning to be conveyed. – Use adjectives and adverbs in sentences and choose between them depending on what is to be modified. *Word Usage* – Use collective nouns and frequently occurring irregular plural nouns. – Use reflexive pronouns. – Form and use the past tense of frequently occurring irregular verbs.
	Grade 3 *Sentence Structure and Meaning* – Produce, expand, and rearrange complete simple, compound, and complex sentences. – Ensure subject-verb and pronoun-antecedent agreement.7 – Use verbs in the present, past, and future tenses and choose among them depending on the overall meaning of the sentence. – Use coordinating and subordinating conjunctions and choose between them depending on the overall meaning of the sentence. – Form and use comparative and superlative adjectives and adverbs and choose between them depending on what is to be modified and the overall meaning of the sentence. *Word Usage* – Use abstract nouns. – Form and use regular and irregular plural nouns and the past tense of regular and irregular verbs.

#2 **Conventions of Capitalization, Punctuation, Spelling** *Demonstrate command of the conventions of standard English capitalization, punctuation, and spelling when writing.*	**Kindergarten** – Capitalize the first word in a sentence and the pronoun I. – Recognize and name end punctuation. – Write a letter or letters for most consonant and short-vowel sounds (phonemes). – Spell simple words phonetically, drawing on knowledge of sound-letter relationships.
	Grade 1 – Capitalize dates and the names of people. – Use end punctuation for sentences. – Capitalize the names of months and people. – Use commas in dates and to separate individual words in a series. – Use conventional spelling for words with common spelling patterns and for frequently occurring irregular words. – Spell untaught words phonetically, drawing on phonemic awareness and spelling conventions.
	Grade 2 – Capitalize holidays, product names, and geographic names. – Use commas in greetings and closings of letters. – Use an apostrophe to form contractions and frequently occurring possessives. – Generalize learned spelling patterns when writing words (e.g., *cage → badge; boy → boil*). – Consult reference materials, including beginning dictionaries, as needed to check and correct spellings.
	Grade 3 – Capitalize appropriate words in titles. – Use commas in addresses. – Use commas and quotation marks in dialogue. – Form and use possessives. – Use conventional spelling for high-frequency and other studied words and for adding suffixes to base words (e.g., *sitting, smiled, cries, happiness*). – Use spelling patterns and generalizations (e.g., word families, position-based spellings, syllable patterns, ending rules, meaningful word parts) in writing words. – Consult reference materials, including beginning dictionaries, as needed to check and correct spellings.

#3 **Knowledge of Language** *Apply knowledge of language to understand how language functions in different contexts, to make effective choices for meaning or style, and to comprehend more fully when reading or listening.*	**Kindergarten** (Begins in Grade 2)
	Grade 1 (Begins in Grade 2)
	Grade 2 Use knowledge of language and its conventions when writing, speaking, reading, or listening. a. Compare formal and informal uses of English.
	Grade 3 Use knowledge of language and its conventions when writing, speaking, reading, or listening. a. Choose words and phrases for effect. b. Recognize and observe differences between the conventions of spoken and written English.
#6 **Academic Vocabulary** *Acquire and use accurately a range of general academic and domain-specific words and phrases sufficient for reading, writing, speaking, and listening at the college and career readiness level; demonstrate independence in gathering vocabulary knowledge.*	**Kindergarten** Use words and phrases acquired through conversations, activities in the kindergarten curriculum, reading and being read to, and responding to texts.
	Grade 1 Use words and phrases acquired through conversations, activities in the grade 1 curriculum, reading and being read to, and responding to texts, including using frequently occurring conjunctions (e.g., *because*).
	Grade 2 Use words and phrases acquired through conversations, activities in the grade 2 curriculum, reading and being read to, and responding to texts, including using adjectives and adverbs to describe.
	Grade 3 Acquire and use accurately grade-appropriate conversational, general academic, and domain-specific words and phrases,8 including those that signal spatial and temporal relationships.

Common Core Speaking and Listening Standards Related to Writing

#1 **Collaborative Conversation** *Prepare for and participate effectively in a range of conversations and collaborations with diverse partners, building on others' ideas and expressing their own clearly and persuasively*	**Kindergarten** Participate in collaborative conversations with diverse partners about kindergarten topics and texts with peers and adults in small and larger groups. – Follow agreed-upon rules for discussions (e.g., listening to others and taking turns speaking about the topics and texts under discussion). – Continue a conversation through multiple exchanges.
	Grade 1 Participate in collaborative conversations with diverse partners about *grade 1 topics and texts* with peers and adults in small and larger groups. – Follow agreed-upon rules for discussions (e.g., listening to others with care, speaking one at a time about the topics and texts under discussion). – Build on others' talk in conversations by responding to the comments of others through multiple exchanges. – Ask questions to clear up any confusion about the topics and texts under discussion.
	Grade 2 Participate in collaborative conversations with diverse partners about *grade 2 topics and texts* with peers and adults in small and larger groups. – Follow agreed-upon rules for discussions (e.g., gaining the floor in respectful ways, listening to others with care, speaking one at a time about the topics and texts under discussion). • Build on others' talk in conversations by linking their comments to the remarks of others. • Ask for clarification and further explanation as needed about the topics and texts under discussion.
	Grade 3 Engage effectively in a range of collaborative discussions (one-on-one, in groups, and teacher-led) with diverse partners on *grade 3 topics and texts*, building on others' ideas and expressing their own clearly. – Come to discussions prepared, having read or studied required material; explicitly draw on that preparation and other information known about the topic to explore ideas under discussion. (See grade 3 Reading Literature Standard 1 and Reading Informational Text Standard 1 for specific expectations regarding use of textual evidence.) – Follow agreed-upon rules for discussions (e.g., gaining the floor in respectful ways, listening to others with care, speaking one at a time about the topics and texts under discussion). – Ask questions to check understanding of information presented, stay on topic, and link their comments to the remarks of others. – Explain their own ideas and understanding in light of the discussion.

#3 **Speaker's Point of View** *Evaluate a speakers point of view, reasoning and use of evidence and rhetoric*	**Kindergarten** Ask and answer questions in order to seek help, get information, or clarify something that is not understood.
	Grade 1 Ask and answer questions about what a speaker says in order to gather additional information or clarify something that is not understood.
	Grade 2 Ask and answer questions about what a speaker says in order to clarify comprehension, gather additional information, or deepen understanding of a topic or issue.
	Grade 3 Ask and answer questions about information from a speaker, offering appropriate elaboration and detail.
#4 **Presenting** *Presenting information, findings, and supporting evidence such that listeners can follow the line of reasoning and the organization, development, and style are appropriate to task, purpose, and audience.*	**Kindergarten** Describe familiar people, places, things and events and with prompting and support, provide additional detail.
	Grade 1 Describe familiar people, places , things and events with relevant details expressing ideas and feelings clearly.
	Grade 2 Tell a story or recount an experience with appropriate facts and relevant, descriptive details, speaking audibly in coherent sentences.
	Grade 3 Report on a topic, tell a story, or recount an experience with appropriate facts and relevant, descriptive details, speaking clearly at an understandable pace.
#6 **Command of Formal English** *Adapt speech to a variety of context and communicative tasks, demonstrating a command of formal English when indicated or appropriate*	**Kindergarten** Speak audibly and express thoughts, feelings and ideas clearly.
	Grade 1 Produce complete sentences when appropriate to task and situation.
	Grade 2 Produce complete sentences when appropriate to task and situation in order to provide requested detail or clarification.
	Grade 3 Speak in complete sentences when appropriate to task and situation in order to provide requested detail or clarification.

Question Cards

Who?

is	did	can	would	will	might

What?

is	did	can	would	will	might

Where?

is	did	can	would	will	might

When?

is	did	can	would	will	might

Why?

is	did	can	would	will	might

How?

is	did	can	would	will	might

Transition Words and Phrases

description	looks like, such as
placement	above, across, behind, below, beside, between, in back of, in front of, near, next to, on top of
compare	alike, both, compared to, just like, in common, same as, similar to
contrast	although, but, however, instead of, on the other hand, unlike
sequence	after, at first, before, beginning with, during, earlier, ending with, finally, first, from then on, last, later, next, second, then, third
cause and effect	as a result, because, because of, caused by, for this reason, leads to, that is why, therefore
to add information	also, another, furthermore, in addition
to conclude	in conclusion, in other words, in short, finally, to conclude
to stress a point	above all, in fact, in other words, most important, to repeat
to provide an example	an example, for example, for instance, such as

Two Column Notes: Three Types of Writing

Informational: Basic

Topic: ______________________________

Main Idea	Facts, Details

Informational: Advanced

Topic:

Main Ideas (1 or 2 words)	Facts, Details, Definitions (words and phrases)
Main Idea 1:	
Main Idea 2:	
Main Idea 3:	

Opinion: Basic

Topic: ____

Opinion	Reasons

Opinion: Advanced

Opinion: ____

Reasons	Details, Examples (words and phrases)
Reason 1:	
Reason 2:	
Reason 3:	

Narrative: Basic

Topic: ______________________________

Event	Details

Narrative: Advanced

Title: ____
Who? ______________________ What?
____
When? _____________________ Where?
____

Events (1 or 2 words)	Details (words and phrases)
Event 1:	
Event 2:	
Event 3:	

Two Column Notes: Patterns of Organization

Description

What I am describing:	
Size	
Shape	
Color	
Location	
Purpose	

Explanation

What I am explaining:	
First	
In addition	
Another	
For example	

Sequence

What I am sequencing:	
First	
Second	
Next	
Then	
Finally	

Cause and Effect

Topic:	
Effect	
Another Effect	
Cause	
Another Cause	

Compare and Contrast

What I am comparing:	
One way they are the same	
Another way they are the same	
One way they are different	
Another way they are different	

Problem and Solution

Topic:	
Problem	
Solution	
Another solution	

Writing Templates: Patterns of Organization

Description/Explanation

Topic sentence:

First:

In addition:

For example:

Concluding sentence:

Sequence

Topic sentence:

First:

Next:

Finally:

Concluding sentence:

Cause and Effect

Topic sentence:

(cause):

That is why:

Another effect is:

Concluding sentence:

Compare and Contrast

Topic sentence:

____

____

____

Compare

One way they are the same:

____

____

____

They both:

____

____

____

Contrast

One way they are different:

____

____

____

Unlike:

____

____

____

Concluding sentence:

____

____

____

Problem and Solution

Topic sentence:

The problem is:

A solution is:

Another solution is:

Concluding sentence:

Examples of Mentor Text *A Ball for Daisy* by Chris Raschka *(wordless story)*

- *A Mama for Owen* by Marion Dane Bauer *(narrative text structure)*
- *An Important Book* by Margaret Wise Brown *(informational text structure)*
- *A Squiggly Story* by Andrew Larsen *(size, style of font, dialogue boxes)*
- *Bat Loves the Night* by Nicola Davies *(informational text structure)*
- *Bears* by Deborah Hodge *(informational text structure)*
- *Brown Bear, Brown Bear What Did You See?* by Bill Martin & Eric Carle *(phrasing)*
- *Bunny Cakes* by Rosemary Wells *(lists)*
- *Cactus Hotel* by Brenda Guiberson *(narrative text)*
- *Carlo Likes Reading* by Jessica Spanyol *(labeling)*
- *Dear Mr. Blueberry* by Simon James *(letter writing)*
- *Duck! Rabbit!* by Amy Krouse Rosenthal *(opinion text structure)*
- *Frog and Toad Together* by Arnold Lobell *(lists)*
- *Good Dog Carl* by Alexandra Day *(wordless story)*
- *Harold and the Purple Crayon* by Crockett Johnson *(drawing)*
- *Hey, Little Ant* by Phillip M. Hoose *(opinion text structure)*
- *How a House is Built* by Gail Gibbons *(informational text structure)*
- *I Don't Want to Be a Frog* by Dave Petty *(dialogue boxes)*
- *In My Opinion* by Deb Bird *(opinion text structure)*
- *Ish* by peter Reynolds *(drawing)*
- *I Wanna Iguana* by Karen Karufman Orloff *(letter writing)*
- *I Want My Hat Back* by Jon Klasses *(voice)*
- *Joshua's Night Whispers* by Angela Johnson *(repeat phrasing)*
- *Meg and Jim's Sled Trip* by Laura Appleton-Smith *(narrative text structure)*
- *My First Books of Planets* by Bruce Betts *(text features)*
- *My Map Book* by Sara Fanelli *(labeling)*
- *Narwhal: Unicorn of the Sea* by Ben Clanton *(drawing)*
- *Not a Box* by Antoinette Portis *(drawing)*
- *Oliver's Must Do List* by Susan Taylor Brown *(lists)*
- *One Word from Sophia* by Jim Averbeck *(opinion text structure)*
- *Owl Moon* by Jane Yolen *(narrative text structure)*
- *Pigeon Has to Go to School* by Mo Willems *(dialogue boxes)*
- *Planting a Rainbow* by Lois Ehlert *(labeling)*
- *Put it on the List* by Kristen Darbyshire *(lists)*
- *Red Rubber Boot Day* by Mary Lyn Ray & Lauren Stringer *(illustration study)*
- *Red is Best* by Kathy Stinson *(opinion text structure)*
- *Say Something* by Peter Reynolds *(voice)*
- *Scaredy Squirrel* by Melanie Watt *(patterns of organization)*
- *Sharks* by Ann Schreiber - National Geographic Kids *(informational text structure)*
- *Sky Color* by Peter Reynolds *(drawing)*
- *Solar System* by Kenneth Walsh *(informational text structure)*
- *Spaceships and Rockets* (DK Readers) *(text features)*
- *Squiggles! A Drawing Book* by Robert Kempe *(drawing)*
- *Stellaluna* by Janell Cannon *(paragraph structure)*
- *Stella Writes an Opinion* by Janiel Wagstaff *(opinion text structure)*
- *Thank You Bear* by Greg Foley *(drawing)*

- *The Bravest Dog Ever: The True Story of Balto* by Natalie Standford *(narrative text structure)*
- *The Dot* by Peter H. Reynolds *(drawing)*
- *The Important Book* by Margaret Wise Brown *("The important thing...)*
- *The Jacket I Wear in the Snow* by Nancy Winslow Parker *(personal narrative)*
- *The Paper Bag Princess* by Robert Munsch *(voice)*
- *The Paperboy* by Dav Pilkey *(narrative text structure)*
- *The Pencil* by Alan Ahlberg *(drawing)*
- *The Perfect Pet* by Margie Palatini *(opinion text structure)*
- *The Popcorn Book* by Tomie DePaola *(dialoge boxes)*
- *The Pumpkin Book* by Gail Gibbons *(labeling)*
- *The Red Book* by Barbara Lehman *(illustration study)*
- *The Snowman* by Raymond Briggs *(wordless story)*
- *This is a Sea Cow* by Cassandra Federman *(conveying attitude)*
- *Wallace's Lists* by Barbara Bottner *(lists)*
- *We Are in a Book* by Mo Willem *(lines and marks to indicate movement)*
- *We Are Water Protectors* by Carole Linstrom & Micaela Goade *(illustration study)*
- *Wemberly Worried* by Kevin Henkes *(voice)*
- *Whales: The Gentle Giants* (Step Into Reading 2) *(paragraph structure)*
- *What Do You Do with a Tail Like This* by Steve Jenkins and Robin Page *(informational text structure)*
- *What is it Like to Be a Fish?* by Wendy Pfeffer *(informational text structure)*
- *XO Ox: A Love Story* by Adam Rex and Scott Campbell *(voice)*
- *Zoom* by Istvan Banyal *(zooming in on a picture)*

References

Academy of Orton-Gillingham. *What is the Orton-Gillingham approach*? Retrieved from https://www.ortonacademy.org/resources/what-is-the-orton-gillingham-approach/

Achieve the Core. *Water Wise: All About Water Conservation.* Retrieved from: https://achievethecore.org/search?q=water+wise

Achieve the Core. *ELA literacy lessons.* Student Achievement Partners. Retrieved from https://achievethecore.org/category/411/ela-literacy-lessons?&g%5B%5D=0&g%5B%5D=1&g%5B%5D=2&sort=name

Adams, M. J. (2011). *Reading, language, and the mind.* Paper presented at the NYSED Network Team Institute, Albany, New York. Retrieved from: www.engageny.org/sites/ default/files/resource/attachments/reading-language-and-the-mind-jager-adams.pdf.

Bangert-Downs, R.L., Kulik, C.C., Kulik, J.A., & Morgan, M. (1991). The instructional effects of feedback in test-like events. *Review of Educational Research, 61 (2)*, 213-238.

Berninger, V. W., & Winn, W. D. (2006). *Implications of Advancements in Brain Research and Technology for Writing Development, Writing Instruction, and Educational Evolution.* In C. A. MacArthur, S. Graham, & J. Fitzgerald (Eds.), *Handbook of writing research* (p. 96–114). The Guilford Press.

Boscolo, P., & Gelati, C. (2007). Best practices in promoting motivation for writing. In S. Graham, C.A. MacArthur, & J. Fitzgerald (Eds.). *Best practices in writing instruction.* New York: Guilford Press.

Burns, M., Griffin, P., Snow, C. (Eds) (1999). *Starting Out Right: A Guide to Promoting Children's Reading Success.* National Academy Press.

Cabell, S.Q., Tortorelli, L.S., & Gerde, H.K. (2013). How do I write: Scaffolding preschoolers' early writing skills. *The Reading Teacher* 66 (8), 650-659.

Calderon, M. (2011). *Teaching Reading and Comprehension to English Learners, K-5.* Bloomington, IN: Solution Tree Press.

Carothers, L. *Sensory words.* Waunakee Community School District, Waunakee, WI. www.waunakee.k12.wi.us/faculty/lcarothers/EffectiveWriting/Descriptive/ Sensory%20Words.pdf

Chapman, M. (2006). Preschool through elementary writing. In P. Smagorinsky (Ed.). *Research on composition: Multiple perspectives on two decades of change.* New York: Teacher College Press.

Coe, M., Hanita, M., Nishioka, V., & Smiley, R. (2011). *An investigation of the impact of the 6+1 Trait Writing model on grade 5 student writing achievement.* (NCEE 2012-4010). Washington, DC: National Center for Education Evaluation and Regional Assistance, Institute of Education Sciences, U.S. Department of Education.

Coker, D. (2007). Writing instruction for young children. In S. Graham, C.A. MacArthur, & J. Fitzgerald (Eds.). *Best practices in writing instruction.* New York: The Guilford Press.

Coker, D. J., & Ritchey, K. D. (2015). *Teaching beginning writers.* New York: The Guilford Press.

Common Core State Standards Initiative (2010). *Common Core State Standards for English language arts and literacy in history/social studies, science, and technical subjects.* Retrieved from www.corestandards.org.

Common Core Standards, *Appendix A: Research supporting key elements of the Standards.* Retrieved from www.corestandards.org/the-standards.

Davies, N. (2001). *One Tiny Turtle.* Somerville, MA: Candlewick Press.

Donovan, C.A., & Smolkin, L.B. (2006). Children's understanding of genre and writing development. In C.A.

MacArthur, S. Graham, & J. Fitzgerald (Eds.), *Handbook of writing research.* New York: Guilford Press.

Duke, N. (2013). Starting out: Practices to use in K-3. *Educational Leadership*, November 2013, 40-44.

Eco Water Canada. *EcoRilla.* Retrieved from https://www.youtube.com/watch?v=_ex1ZuKFw64

Foorman, B., Coyne, M., Denton, C.A., Dimino, J., Hayes, L. Justice, L., Lewis, W., & Wagner, R. (2016). *Foundational skills to support reading for understanding in kindergarten through 3rd grade.* U.S. Department of Education, Institute of Education Sciences. ies.ed.gov/ncee/wwc/practiceguide/21

Gentry, J.R. (1982). An analysis of developmental spelling. *The Reading Teacher*, 36, 192- 200.

Gentry, J.R. (2007). *The stages of spelling development for kindergarten.* Zaner-Bloser. Retrieved from: bpsassets.weebly.com/uploads/9/9/3/2/9932784/gentry.pdf.

Geiger, A., (2014, April 16). *Teaching tips for children in different stages of writing development.* Retrieved from: www.themeasuredmom.com/stages-of-writing-development- help-kids-move/.

Glover, M (2014). Vision and choice in the K-3 writing workshop. In Ganske, K. (Ed). *Write now! Empowering writers in today's K-6 classroom.* Newark, DE: International Reading Association.

Graham, S., Bollinger, A., Booth O., C., D'Aoust, C., MacArthur, C., McCutchen, D., & Olinghouse, N. (2012). *Teaching elementary students to be effective writers: A practice guide* (NCEE 2012-4058). Washington, DC: National Center for Education Evaluation and Regional Assistance, Institute of Education Sciences, U.S. Department of Education. Retrieved from ies.ed.gov/ncee/wwc/publications-reviews.aspx#pubsearch.

Graham, S., Moats, L., Neuman, S. (2008). *Teaching writing.* Retrieved from: www.readingrockets.org/webcasts/3001

Graham, S. & Harris, K.R. (2002). Prevention and intervention for struggling writers. In M.R. Shinn, H.M. Walker, & G. Stoner (Eds.). *Interventions for academic and behavior problems: Preventive and remedial approaches.* Bethesda, MD: National Association of School Psychologists.

Graham, S., & Hebert, M. (2010). *Writing to read: Evidence for how writing can improve reading.* A Carnegie Corporation Time to Act Report. Washington, DC:Alliance for Excellent Education.

Graham, S. (2009-2010). Want to improve children's writing? Don't neglect their handwriting. *American Educator*, Winter 2009-2010.

Graham, S., Harris, K.R., & Santangelo, T. (2015). Research-based writing practices and the Common Core: Meta-analysis and meta-synthesis. *The Elementary School Journal 115* (4). (pp. 498-522

Graham, S., & Perin, D. (2007). *Writing next: Effective strategies to improve writing of adolescents in middle and high schools – A report to Carnegies Corporation of New York.* Washington, DC: Alliance for Excellent Education.

Graham, S., & Santangelo, T. (2014). Does spelling instruction make students better speller, readers, and writers? A meta-analystic review. *Reading and Writing,* 1-41.

Graves, D.H. (1989). Writing: Teachers and children at work. In D.S. Strickland & L.M. Morrow (Eds.) *Emergent literacy: Young children learn to read and write.* Newark, DL: International Reading Association.

Hall, A. H. (2014). Beyond the author's chair. *The Reading Teacher* 68 (1), pp 27-31. 302

Hanna, P.R., Hodges, P.R., Hanna, J.L & Rudolph, E.H. (1966). *Phoneme-grapheme correspondences as cues to spelling improvement.* Washington, DC: U.W. Office of Education.

Harris, K., & Graham, S. (1996). *Making the writing process work: Strategies for composition and self-regulation* (2nd ed.). Cambridge, MA: Brookline Books.

Harris, K. R., Graham, S., & Mason, L. H. (2003). *Self-regulated strategy development in the classroom: Part of a balanced approach to writing instruction for students with disabilities.* Focus on Exceptional Children, 35(7), 1-16.

Harris, K. R., Graham, S., & Mason, L. H. (2006). *Improving the writing, knowledge, and motivation of struggling young writers: Effects of self-regulated strategy development with and without peer support.* American Educational Research Journal, 43, 295-340.

Harris, K. R., Graham, S., Mason, L. H., & Fiedlander, B. (2008). *POWERFUL Writing strategies for all students.* Baltimore, MD: Brookes.

Harris, K. R., & Graham, S. (2017). Self-regulated strategy development: Theoretical bases, critical instructional elements, and future research. In R. Fidalgo & T. Olive (Series Eds.) & R. Fidalgo, K. R. Harris, & M. Braaksma (Vol. Eds.), *Studies in Writing: Vol. 34, Design Principles for teaching effective writing: Theoretical and empirical grounded principles* (pp. 119–151). Leiden, nl: Brill Editions.

Hayes, J.R., & Flower, L. (1980). Identifying the organization of writing processes. In L.W. Gregg & E.R. Steinberg (Eds.), *Cognitive processes in writing: An interdisciplinary approach* (pp. 3-30). Hillsdale, NJ: Erlbaum.

Hayes J.R. (1996). A new framework for understanding cognition and affect in writing. In C.M. Levy & S. Ransdell (Eds.) *The science of writing: Theories, methods, individual differences and applications* (pp. 1-27). Mahwah, NJ: Erbaum.

Hayes, J.R. (2004). What triggers revision? In L. Allal, L. Chanquoy, & P. Largy (Eds.), *Studies in writing: Vol. 13. Revision: Cognitive and instructional processes* (pp. 9-20). Norwell, MA Kluwer.

Haynes, C., & Maxwell, L. From talking to writing: strategies for supporting narrative expository expression. PowerPoint presentation. Retreived from https://docplayer.net/76174335-From-talking-to-writing-strategies-for-supporting-narrative-and-expository-expression-preschool-and-school-age-methods.html

Hidi, S., & Boscolo, P. (2006). Motivation and writing. In C.A. MacArthur, S. Graham, & J. Fitzgerrald (Eds.). *Handbook of Writing Research.* New York: Guilford Press.

Hillocks, G. (1986). *Research on written composition, new directions for teaching.* ERIC Clearninghouse. eric.ed.gov/?id=ED265552

Jennings, T., & Haynes, C.W. (2002). *From talking to writing: Strategies for scaffolding expository expression.* Prides Crossing MA: Landmark Outreach Program.

Kim, Y.S., Al Otaiba, S., Puranik, C., Folsom, J.S>, Greulich. L., & Wagner, R.K. (2011). Componential skills of beginning writing: An exploratory study. *Learning and Individual Differences,* 21, 517-525.

Lonigan, C. & Shanahan, T. (2008). *Developing early literacy: Report of the National Early Literacy Panel.* Washington, DC: National Institute for Literacy.

MacArthur, C. A. (2007). Best practices in teaching evaluation and revision. In S. Graham, C.A. MacArthur, & J. Fitzgerald (Eds.). *Best practices in writing instruction.* New York: Guilford Press.

McKenzie, L., & Tomkins, G.E. (1984). Evaluating students' writing: A process approach. *Journal of Teaching Writing* 3 (2) 201-212.

Mehta, P.D., Foorman, B.R., Martin, L., & Taylor, W.P. (2005). Literacy as a unidimensional multilevel construct: Validation sources of influence and implications in a longitudinal study in grades 1 to 4. *Scientific Studies of Reading, 9* (2), 85-116.

Moorman, H. (2010, November 10). *Stages of writing development.* Retrieved from: www.slideshare.net/hmoorman/stages-of-writing-development.

Myhill, D., & Jones, S. (2009). How talk becomes text: Investigating the concept of oral rehearsal in early years' classrooms. *British Journal of Educational Studies 57* (3). 265-284.

National Council of Teachers of English (NCTE). What we know about writing, grades K-2. Retrieved 2016 from: https://ncte.org/writing/aboutearlygrades

National Governors Association Center for Best Practices & Council of Chief State School Officers. (2010). *Common Core State Standards*. Washington, DC: Authors.

Neuman, S.B., & Wright, T.S. (2013). *All about words: Increasing vocabulary in the Common Core classroom, Pre-K-2.* New York, NY: Teachers College Press.

O'Connor, C. (2012). *Academically productive talk: Discussion within Word Generation.* PowerPoint presentation, Baltimore Summer Institute, August 15, 2012.

NICHH National Institute of Child Health and Human Development. (2000). *Report of the National Reading Panel. Teaching children to read: An evidence-based assessment of the scientific research literature on reading and its implications for reading instruction* (NIH Publication No. 00-4769). Washington, DC: U.S. Government Printing Office.

Paris, S.G., & Hamilton, E.E. (2009). The development of children's reading comprehension. In S.E. Israel & G.G. Duffy (Eds.). *Handbook of research on reading comprehension.* New York: Routledge.

Pearson, P.E., & Gallagher, M.C. (1983). The instruction of reading comprehension. *Contemporary Educational Psychology*, 8, 317-344.

Pennington, B., McGrath, F., Lauren, M., & Peterson, R.L. (2019). *Diagnosing learning disorders: From science to practice 3rd edition.* New York: The Guilford Press.

Pritchard, R.J., & Honeycutt, R.L. (2007). Best practices in implementing a process approach to teaching writing. In S. Graham, C.A. MacArthur, & J. Fitzgerald (Eds.), *Best practices in writing instruction.* New York: Guilford Press.

Ramirez, B. (2006). *Star of the Day: Jordan.* Unpublished student manuscript, 1st grade. Myford Elementary, Tustin Unified School District, Irvine, CA.

Ray, K. W. (2010). *In pictures and in words.* Portsmouth, NH: Heinemann.

Reading Rockets. *Literacy centers.* Retrieved from: https://www.readingrockets.org/article/literacy-centers.

Regan, K. & Mastropieri, M.A. (2009). *A focus on self regulated strategy development (SRSD) for writing.* Teaching LD.org, Division for Learning Disabilities and Division for Research of the Council for Exceptional Children: Current Practice Alert, Issue 17.

Reutzel, P., Mohr, K.A.J., & Jones, C. D. (2017). Exploring the relationship between letter recognition and handwriting in early literacy development. *Journal of Early Childhood Literacy. 19* (3) 349-374.

Rodier, A. (2000). A cure for writer's block: Writing for real audiences. *The Quarterly, 22* (2).

Roth, K. & Dabrowski, J. (2014). Extending interactive writing into Grades 2-5. *The Reading Teacher, 68* (1), 33-44. Retrieved from Reading Rockets: https://www.readingrockets.org/article/extending-interactive-writing-grades-2-5

Routman, R., (2005) *Writing Essentials.* Portsmouth, NH: Heinemann.

Routman, R. (2014). *Read, write, lead.* Alexandria, VA: ASCD.

Saddler, B. & Preschern, J. (2007). Improving sentence writing ability through sentence- combining practice. *Teaching Exceptional Children*, 39 (3), 6-11.

Saddler, B. (2012). *Teacher's guide to effective sentence writing.* NY: Guilford Press.

Salt Lake City School District: *Developmental writing continuum.* Retrieved from: www. slcschools.org/departments/assessment-and-evaluation/documents/Writing-Continuum. pdf

Sanders, T.J.M. & Schilpernoord, J. (2006). Text structure as a window on the cognition of writing: How text analysis provides insights. In C.A. MacArthur, S. Graham, & J. Fitzgerald (Eds.), *Handbook of writing research.* New York: Guilford Press.

Scott, C. (2004). Syntactic contributions to literacy development. In C. Stone, E. Stillman, B. Ehren, & K. Apel (Eds.), *Handbook of language and literacy* (pp. 340-362). New York: Guilford Press.

Sedita, J. (2013, 2015). *Keys to Content Writing.* Rowley, MA: Keys to Literacy.

Sedita, J. (2003, 2015) *The Key Comprehension Routine, Primary Grades.* Rowley, MA: Keys to Literacy.

Sedita, J. (2019). *The Writing Rope: The Strands That Are Woven into Skilled Writing.* Rowley, M: Keys to Literacy.

Shanahan, T., Callison, K., Carriere, C., Duke, N.K., Pearson, P.D., Schatschneider, C., & Torgesen, J. (2010). *Improving reading comprehension in kindergarten through 3rd grade: A practice guide* (NCEE 2010-4038). Washington, DC: National Center for Education Evaluation and Regional Assistance, Institute of Education Sciences, U.S. Department of Education.

Snow, C., Griffin, P., & Burns, M.S. (2005). *Knowledge to support the teaching of reading: Preparing teachers for a changing world.* San Francisco: Josey-Bass.

Spandel, V. (2009). *Creating writers through 6-trait writing assessment and instruction.* New York: Pearson.

Strong, W. (1986). *Creative approaches to sentence combining.* ERIC Clearinghouse on Reading ad Communication Skills. National Council of Teachers of English.

Taylor, S.P. (2008). *A quick guide to persuasive writing.* Heinemann Educational Books.

Trupiano, C. (2006). Best classroom practices. In A. Horning & A. Becker (Eds). *Revision: history, theory, and practices.* Parlor Press.

Walberg, H.J. (1999). Productive teaching. In H.C. Waxman & H.J. Walberg (Eds.). *New directions for teaching practice and research.* 75-104. Berkeley, CA: McCutchin Publishing Corporation.

Waunakee Community School District. *Sensory word list.* Retrieved from: https://www.waunakee.k12.wi.us/faculty/lcarothers/EffectiveWriting/Descriptive/Sensory%20Words.pdf

Wiggins, G. (1993). *Assessing student performance: Exploring the purpose and limits of testing.* San Francisco: Josey-Bass.

Wiggins, G. (2012). Seven keys to effective feedback. *Educational Leadership*, 70, (1), pages 10-16.

Witte, S. (2013). Preaching what we practice: A study of revision. *Journal of Curriculum and Instruction* 6(2), 33-59.